She Strategy

JULIA AQUINO-SERRANO

ELITE PRODUCTIONS
INSPIRE. ASPIRE. IMPACT.

Published by: EliteFoundationAuthorAcademy®,Ft Lauderdale,FL.

EliteFoundationAuthorAcademy® is a registered trademark.

Edited by: Patricia Nolan, About the Words

Photography: Graciela Valdes

Illustrator: Amy Parker, AP Designworks, Inc

Printed in the United States of America.

ISBN: 978-1-7293926-1-4

This publication is designed to provide accurate and authoritative information regarding the subject matter covered. It is sold with the understanding that the publisher is not engaged in rendering legal, accounting, clinical or other professional advice. If legal advice or other expert assistance is required, the services of a competent professional should be sought. The opinions expressed by the authors in this book are not endorsed by: EliteFoundationAuthorAcademy® and are the sole responsibility of the author rendering the opinion.

Most EliteFoundationAuthorAcademy® titles are available at for bulk purchases for sales promotions, premiums, fundraising, and educational use. Special versions or book excerpts can also be created on direct request for specific needs aligned with Elite.

For more information, please write:
EliteFoundationAuthorAcademy®
2003 West Cypress Creek Road, Ste. 103 Ft. Lauderdale, Florida 33369

Or email: ElitePublisher@EliteFundsFreedom.org

Visit us online at:
www.Eliteperformanceacademy.us/elite-book-creation-publishing-services/

FOREWORD

n an age of so many paradoxical paradigms of thought, each proliferating the world with its beliefs and views, Author Julia Aquino-Serrano offers a refreshing application of truth. A truth she gained personal experience and that is transparently shared for your benefit.

It is the authenticity of the expression and guidance offered by Mrs. Aquino-Serrano that is so empowering. She eloquently distills complex and seemingly complicated life dilemmas and encourages the reader to do the work that is predicated on fundamental knowledge of what it means to be centered on self-first, to enhance responsibility for living life on one's terms, rather than allowing life to live you.

She shares how life's setbacks, undoubtedly will occur, and offers her solution.

The solution is to exercise your free-will, now.

Choice is a central theme in Julia Aquino-Serrano's writings. It may appear at first glance as common sense, but through intentional deep reflection and ponderance, we all can identify with a time in life when we were presented with making a choice and either became frozen in existence, passive or exercised it.

Author Julia Aquino-Serrano impresses that it is this ability to remain open to possibilities and to behave in a manner that supports self-actualization that is paramount to transformation. She shares her personal journey of departing from the predisposition of potential addiction, the toxicity in personal relationships, and a triumph over all that could have influenced her life, to take on a very different path.

Through her literary work, Julia pours out her learnings, to empower you, the reader, to take action on your journey, towards becoming an active participant in creating your life's dreams. She not only provides her roadmap, but aligns herself with you, to share how she overcame challenges that can prevent you from evolving.

This is a must read and a call to act, to create your SheStrategy, to live an enriched and fulfilling life.

Dr. Jessica L. Vera, Ph.D.
Multiple Bestselling Award-Winning Author
CEO, Authentic Living LLC
Founder, Elite Foundation
501(c)(3) nonprofit dedicated to **A Future for Every Survivor**
drj@drjvera.com
info@EliteFundsFreedom.org

REVIEWS

S he Strategy: A Guide to Disrupting Limiting Beliefs and Creating A Plan for a Lifetime of Success! is definitely one those "change your life" books. Julia starts the book with examples and actions steps to help you understand your current mindset and how best to shift it so that it better serves you. This book forces you to conduct a reality check and take a hard look in the mirror. By reading her approach and doing the exercises in the book on this fundamental concept of self-aware-ness, I realized that I was telling myself stores that had no real basis. If I changed those stores from limiting to limitless, I could improve both my personal and professional life dramatically. I realized that I could increase the time I spent with my family and also pursue other personal goals as well. The second part of the book was my favorite because it made you put pen to paper and takes you on a journey to clarify what you want to achieve. Julia forces you to dig deep and really understand your values and how they play out in your life goals. The book finishes by helping you bridge mindset and goals with a plan to get real results. Throughout the book, I felt like I had a coach, therapist and consultant on a very powerful self-realization journey. I strongly suggest this book to everyone!

-Kavita Sahai, CEO 21drops

From her opening statement, Julia draws you in. She lets you know that all you need to achieve your goals, regardless of what they are, is something that is already within you. That alone is empowering. But she goes on. This book is not just about helping you to achieve your goals, but also to help you become a better version of yourself. No matter where you are in your life, Julia assures you that it is never too late to start. It is okay to shine and to find your power. You learn that you are okay as you are, and that you must accept others as they are. Through sharing her personal childhood experiences, Julia explains that regardless of your upbringing, your life is defined by the choices you make now. *SheStrategy* is an eye opening, heart and soul opening must read for all women.

-Lisa J. Hauser, Executive Consultant

   In SheStrategy, Julia walks us through her own struggles to dispel the demons of her past and step into a new life - one she is proud of, happy with, and deeply grateful for. Leaving behind the traditional trappings of "success," she dug deep and had the courage to adjust her goals and behavior to be more in line with her true purpose and values. She discovered the key components that ensured a positive outcome. She wrote SheStrategy so that other women could benefit from her experience. It is a powerful book that proves that with a mindset shift, focused action, and conscious choice, everything is possible. SheDefine your life today with SheStrategy!

-Patricia Nolan of About the Words

DEDICATION

This book is being dedicated in memory of Sheryl Valency. Sheryl was a bright light who left us too soon. After Sheryl's surgery to treat her Glioblastoma, a deadly form of brain cancer, her first words to me were "Jules, I get it now! We have to live from the inside. It's who we are inside, not outside. We already have what we need."

Yes, my friend. Yes.

Rest in Peace, Sheryl and thank you for your unconditional love, friendship, and inspiration to finish this book.

PERSONAL NOTE

wrote She Strategy to bring both awareness of what holds us back and a simple process to living your best life, removing overwhelm and the feeling of helplessness, hopelessness, or both.

She Strategy is a tool; a guide to get us out of our own head and to take intentional action to build a life we desire. Use it to move you forward and to find the confidence of your value and your innate gifts. Use it to create intentionally. Acknowledge what comes up. Allow it to exist. And, make change where you are ready to make change. Be patient.

Remember that the real work, the actual success, the awareness and the change begins and ends with you. I believe that we have the gift of our lifetime to learn, grow, expand, build, and live. In this lifetime, one of those lessons is the acknowledgment of our deeper truth and purpose. In that learning, we shift from ego-driven beliefs and thoughts to living an authentic, consciously designed life.

My hope for you is that you find your soul's purpose and live your destined life. Be open to the failures that lead to powerful learning and the success that follows. Find acceptance of "what is" to live in the present moment and make conscious choices that align with who you are – not who the world has defined you to be.

And, my greater vision is that you find your way to the truth of the power that you possess, the innate gifts you've been given, and the open heart required to love yourself in an imperfect world designed to provide the most perfect life.

In gratitude and love…Julia

She Strategy® is a program available through SheDefined.com.

_____

SheDefined.com offers coaching, retreats, and workshops for women who wish to change their world, desire success and a life lived on their terms. It's for women who want to live from a place of authenticity, self-love, and continuous learning and growth

CONTENTS

INTRODUCTION

> *Change your thoughts and you change your world.*
> —Norman Vincent Peale

ave you ever had one of those days, weeks, months, years, where you think, "Is this really my life? My career? My family? My fate?" We all have. We wonder, "Is this really what life is all about?" "Is this all there is?"

The answer is a booming outside voice NO…unless you believe that this is all there is, then *yes*, this *is* all there is to life…if that is what you choose. But if you desire something different, you *can* make a change. You can shift your mindset and take a step forward. You can make a different choice. You can reframe your perspective. See the other side. Accept life as it is today, and choose consciously to create your future. So, if you've asked yourself those questions and are seeking answers, then you are in the right place.

This book is the common sense approach to changing your reality through conscious choice and focused action. It's about living your life consciously, by design, based on *your* definition of what your life should represent.

I call it a SheDefined life.

I've got solutions, guidance, and a bit of She Strategy to help you. But, and it may be a big "but", you have to be willing to do something different, to "be" your greatness, to let go of some limiting beliefs, to walk through fear, and to take focused, determined, intentional action.

So, how are we going to get to the realization of our dreams? Our deepest desires? Our greatest power? How will we fulfill our destiny using our greatest gifts?

I have a secret to share with you. Actually, it's a big *mystery*. I'm going to reveal it right up front. I call it a mystery because somehow, we don't know it or we don't believe it to be true. But it is true. And it is our greatest gift. Are you ready?

Here it is. Take a deep breath, slowly breathe out…and read the next line - the truth.

You have everything you need, right now, inside of you, to create any life you truly desire. That power, which is your gift, comes from within. Not. From. Without. It comes from the inside-out, not from the outside-in.

Let me clarify this. You have the strength, intelligence, fortitude, vision, ability, resources, creativity, and courage to do whatever you choose, and to be whomever you desire. It is inside of you right now. It is inherent in your nature. You were born with it. It does not need to be found. It just needs to be uncovered.

What you must do is tap into it. Become aware of your power. Find gratitude for your gifts. Be willing to act! *It takes both awareness and willingness.* You must do whatever it takes to get to *that place* you keep saying you want to go. To be that person you want to be - the person you choose to be. The person you were meant to be: joyful, peaceful, generous, happy, open, loving, kind, healthy, prosperous, graceful, and abundant.

In the process, you will have to let go of your tightly held limiting beliefs and ego-serving mindset. You must be willing to let go of fear and be open to find love and to give love.

You will need to forgive others and, more importantly, forgive yourself. You will have to be courageous enough to change your mindset and take a leap of faith. You will be required to believe that you are capable and strong beyond your wildest dreams. You will have to truly believe that you were made perfectly and born with everything you need to live your life with purpose and on-purpose. You must begin to believe in you.

Always remember: You are enough. This book, this work, is not about "fixing" you. I cannot fix you because you are not broken. This isn't about doing more or even better. This is about living your life on your terms because it is your life.

Open your heart. Open your mind. Take a deep breath and start from *now*. Now is different for everyone. This book will lead you to your *now*, which is the perfect and *only* moment for you to choose, believe, and act. The transformation will be based on you and what you are willing to do. You are in control of what happens in this moment because you are also responsible for your thoughts, your actions, and your mindset at this moment. Your now is your new beginning. It doesn't need to look like anyone else's *now*, and it doesn't need to be right this moment. However, if you are reading this book, there is something you are seeking. So, this is where we will start, from *now*.

Truth Alert: **This book will lead, guide, and inspire you to the greatness that is already within you. No one else can create the life of your dreams except you. No one else can change your life except you. If I could, I would. If your mom, spouse, or friend could do it for you, they would too! But they can't. Heck, they may not have been able to do it for themselves, yet. So, it is on you. Now is your moment to commit to taking a walk down the rocky path that will lead you to your greatness. Own it. It will be worth it.**

Before we dive in, I'd like to share a quote from Marianne Williamson's influential book, A Return To Love. It's one of my favorites. Read it one sentence at a time. Breathe it in. Allow it to seep into your pores. And, then, read it once again.

Our deepest fear is not that we are inadequate. Our deepest fear is that we are powerful beyond measure. It is our light, not our darkness thaᲮm st fr ghtens us.

We ask ourselves, "Who am I to be brilliant, gorgeous, talented, fabulous?"

Actually, who are you *not* to be? *You* are a child of God. Your playing small does not serve the world. There is nothing enlightened about shrinking so that other people won't feel insecure around you. We are all meant to shine, as children do. We were born to make manifest the glory of God that is within us. It is not just in some of us; it's in *everyone*. And, as we let our own light shine, we unconsciously give other people permission to do the same. As we are liberated from our own fear, our presence automatically liberates others.

My wish for you is that you find your power and shine your light.

Remember, this is a journey and there will be twists and turns along the road. There will be jagged edges, leaps forward, unexpected cliffs, and everything in between. Take your time. Be kind to yourself. Be gentle. *Love* yourself and your journey. Remember you can do this; your love and your power is unlimited.

So, let's go! Let's SheDefine your life starting *now*.

SECTION 1

STARTING FROM WHERE WE ARE

n coaching and in life, to truly benefit from our relationships, we must meet people where THEY are. However, we mostly meet people from where WE are. What does this mean? We tend to expect people to have our beliefs, our mindset, our experiences, our knowledge. And, as a result, we expect that they will think like we do; act like we do; respond to life as we respond to life. And, when they don't, we judge them. We judge them for where they are in life, for what they believe or how they think. We judge them for being further along or not as far along as we are. We judge them on how they dress, how they walk, how they talk, or even how they carry themselves.

On the other hand, when we meet people where THEY are, we meet them from acceptance of who they are in that moment. We meet them without judgment and with an open heart to their experiences that have brought them to who they are in this moment. We meet them with curiosity and kindness. We meet them in non-judgment. I know it is easier said than done.

The significance of this insight is that we must, in this section of the book, meet ourselves where WE are—today, in this moment. In acceptance of what is. Without judgment. Without regret. Instead, we must take these next steps with an open, loving, accepting, kind, and forgiving heart. We must start with love first. Love of ourselves. Acceptance of where we are. Acknowledgement of the path that has created the lessons and the learning.

We must start from where we are to create the path to where we wish to go. And, to gain an understanding of where we are, let's start with the stories we tell.

Buckle in....it will be worth it!

CHAPTER 1:

MY STORY

was born in Hialeah, an exciting city in Miami, and grew up during an interesting time. It was during a growth boom and Hialeah, and Miami became the settlement area for many Cuban migrants during the "Marielito" Boatlift in 1980—where 125,000 Cuban refugees were sent to the United States in overcrowded boats, with no regard for their safety by the Cuban government.

It was an interesting time because Hialeah was mostly a very American population at the time. A population that was Nationalistic at heart. The influx of Cuban immigrants was influential to our town, and in our families life. This immigration was important because I grew up in a home with parental figures who I will describe as prejudiced and racist. I remember, at a very young age, getting upset when my brother-in-law referred to a black man as the 'N' word. I asked him not to use that word. I was eight years old and, let's say, he didn't (and still doesn't) respect my request.

Well, his prejudice was not limited to the color of someone's skin, but also to the language they spoke, the way they "looked", and their family origins. It was deeply ingrained from his childhood and through his upbringing— but ultimately, it was a choice. I had a deep sense that his way of *being* was harmful to the world, and it hurt me in a way I could not describe at my young age. I realize now, that *sense* was my instinct; my knowing. His prejudice affected our relationship because I fought him and his beliefs my entire life, and although he treated me like one of his daughters, I never fully trusted his love nor respected his truth.

My home growing up was unique because it consisted of 3 parental figures: my mom, my sister, and my brother-in-law. My sister was 20 years older than I was, so she was a "parent" to me. Our home consisted of her two children - my niece and my nephew, myself, and their child together who was born when I was six years old and my niece and nephew were 6 and 8. Every other weekend, my "step" niece and nephew would come over and then we were a family of 9, living in an 800 square foot home, with three bedrooms and one bathroom.

It was a working-class home. My mom stayed home during the week while my sister and brother-in-law worked. She took care of the house and was there when we came back from school every day. There were fresh-baked cookies and snacks and dinner on the table every night. Saturdays were "chore" days. And, on Sundays, our house was filled with people, football, and lots and lots of beer.

They were doing the best they could, to raise the family with both what they knew and what they had. I remember an exceptional dish that my mom would make. None of my friends had ever had this dish. It was a delicacy, I figured. It was mashed potatoes on toast. It was one of my favorite meals. I only found out later that it was a family meal because potatoes would go a long way on a short budget and it would feed a large family. They did the very best with what they had.

It was a drinking and smoking home. A home full of fun and dysfunction. We were on a collision-course with life that would leave much destruction and pain, but, in perspective, allowed for learning and love.

There was as much dysfunction as there was love. All three parental figures drank alcohol daily. They were what is referred to as "functioning" alcoholics, although they would never describe themselves that way. It was Beer-thirty when they arrived home from work. It was a ritual. They would come home, shower, get comfortable, grab a beer and another cigarette. Often, when I was in my room, I would only know they were home when I heard the click-

click of the pop-top on the beer. They would drink and smoke until they went to bed. It was our normal. I thought all families were like this.

My mom, on the other hand, was mostly functioning, but she also would binge drink. When she would shift from drinking beer to drinking hard liquor, she would become fall-down drunk. Those moments are the most devastating emotional moments I can remember. Those are stand-out moments in my life. I loved her so completely that there was never judgment of her drinking, but instead emotional pain and much fear about when she was going to shift from beer to liquor. *I managed my anxiety around her drinking through trying to manage her.* This is where I learned "control". It was a lot for a child to take on. I would try anything to distract her from making another drink or making the switch to liquor.

I remember one summer we were in Michigan together, where she grew up. We were at a party with my Aunt and Uncle—who I adored. I was around thirteen years old. Someone offered my mom a scotch. She said yes! Then another. Then another. I begged her not to have anymore. Her sister, my aunt, took me aside and told me to shut my mouth, and then went and made my mom an even stronger drink. Let's say it was a bad night. It took me a long time to forgive my aunt, and my heart continued to cry out for my mom.

My love for my mom was unconditional. We were very close. I could tell her anything. And, I mean *anything*. She just listened, without judgment. And, she loved everyone. Because of her big and open heart, we often had strangers on the couch; people who needed a place to stay while they were figuring something out. She was a powerful woman who had her own struggles growing up. She tended to be open to other's path as their own, so she judged less and loved more. But, everyone knew not to cross a line with her. She was fiercely protective, and she is the first person I heard tell a man who had crossed a line: "Don't confuse my kindness with weakness. There's the door."

As a child of an alcoholic, you learn co-dependence rather quickly. You learn to try to keep the peace because it staves off anger. You learn to be "perfect" to make them happy. You learn to think 20 steps ahead and "see" 100 miles up the road to prevent mistakes and head off any problems. *Your need for control becomes more significant than your need for food and water.*

You learn to build a wall around your heart that is formed of steel and reinforced by titanium. You learn to hide your tears and remain stoic in the face of anything and everything. You learn that in fight or flight, your only option is to stay and fight. Until that moment when you can't take it anymore, and then you take flight, only to have your co-dependence lead you back— like a moth to a flame.

My brothers' addictions started from drugs and moved into alcohol as they aged. They were also 18 and 22 years older than me. They were both such gentle, loving souls—and so funny! But, as I got older and as my armor became stronger, I walked away, physically and emotionally. I could no longer continue to be in the same room with them and watch them become incoherent, barely able to walk from their drinking. It broke my heart, every single time, into 1,000 little pieces. And, so, I ran. They missed out on me and I missed out on them. A real tragedy, but somehow necessary on my path.

Through it all, none of them won their battle with alcoholism and addiction, a disease that destroys lives and entire families, if left untreated. I went to my first Al-Anon meeting in my teens and learned the wisdom of AA (Alcoholics Anonymous). It may have been the basis for my desire to go deeper, to find a way to deal with my demons, to accept and to let go, and, ultimately, to respect my path as mine to own, and to allow their paths to be theirs to own.

My life's story is essential to this book because it informed so much of my past, and the lessons learned inform so much of my now. The pain, the fear, the suffering, the love, the fun, the happiness, the devastation, the sadness, the tears, all went into who I am today. However, the most significant determinant of my *now* are my choices through it all.

This shared personal history is just a glimpse into my story. There is much more to my story as there is to yours. We are complex beings, with baggage, beliefs, values, stories, pain, love, fear, courage and scars as a result of our experiences that result in our Story.

Truth Alert: **The important lesson though is that it's not the story that creates our life; it's what we do with our story that matters. Our story can define us or we can define it.**

I still feel both pain and love when I look back. I can now see the purpose of it all and am grateful for the lessons that were learned. I have done a lot of work to let go of my judgment of what happened and to take back my life and to own the outcomes. I have grown deeply and realize that there is always work to be done. It has not been easy, and I continue to work to be a better person, to learn, to grow, to say I'm sorry, to forgive (myself and others), and to choose. I am grateful for it all because in my search for my inner truth, I am moving towards my chosen life. My dreams, my goals, my peaceful self— my destined life of purpose and love.

And, many of those lessons ar e a part of this book—intended to serve the greater good and to bring awareness to our gifts, our innate greatness and our soul's desire for an intentional life.

CHAPTER 2:
AWARENESS
THE DOORWAY TO YOUR SELF

> *Rather than being your thoughts and emotions, be the awareness behind them.*
>
> *—Eckhart Tolle*

Awareness is the crucial first step toward creating the life we desire and the life that is right for us. It is the secret sauce that will help us SheDefine our lives. Without awareness, we cannot change anything effectively or intentionally. It is the mental springboard of progress. Within the definition of awareness, we find words like knowledge, realization, perception, and consciousness. These are interchangeable words we want in abundance in our lives. We can never be too aware. So, let's focus inward and see what we find. But first, we'll briefly examine the opposite of awareness.

Too often, we are operating unconsciously, or unaware. We go through our day on autopilot. We are robotic in our thoughts and actions. We feel detached and even empty. We are operating without awareness.

It seems impossible, but we've all experienced driving on the highway at a high rate of speed and arriving at our destination with only a spotty recollection of the journey. We've been down the path so many times; we can make it almost anywhere without being fully present. Think about it; we can be driving and entirely miss our exit for the same reason, because we lack awareness. Driving without presence and intention is a real-life example that is dangerous to our physical bodies, and reflective of an all-too-common state of mind.

There are dozens of examples in our daily lives. The times we are having a conversation on our cell phone and wondering where our cell phone is. I have had numerous cell phone conversations with my husband while asking him to give me a minute to find my phone! We chalk these events up to mind clutter and stress and laugh them off as part of life. But in reality, these are the symptoms of a more significant issue. A lack of awareness keeps us from growing and making progress. Our lack of self-awareness holds us back from living a purposeful existence.

How about the times when we speak thoughtlessly? The times when we say hurtful or rude things that we wish we could take back? These harsh words tumble out in a moment of fury or frustration. They are unconscious words, but once said cannot be unsaid. They do damage to the person hearing them and to the person who uttered them. These words come from a lack of self-awareness and awareness of others. They are words spoken, without thought, or from negative thoughts, judgments, and feelings (unconsciously operating, in the background).

Have you ever been embarrassed because someone just told you something meaningful and personal and two minutes later in your conversation, you ask a question that was previously answered? It's like getting called-out. The person knows that you were engaging in mindless conversation, and worse, weren't even listening to what they were telling you. You feel awful. You know yourself to be giving and caring, however, at that moment you miss out on the opportunity to be giving and caring because you were operating "unconsciously"; living inside your mind. Without awareness, you will continue to have those cringe-worthy moments over and over and may miss the opportunity to learn, grow, or provide insight, guidance, or a listening ear to help another.

Now, take a step away from the daily examples of un-awareness and take a good look at your life as a whole. How often do you say things like, "How did I get here?" or "How did my life get to this point?" How much of your life feels like it has merely "happened" to you? How much of your life is the result of what could be defined as "bad choices"? Take a serious introspective look. We can SheDefine a bad choice as a choice that was made while lacking awareness. That's it. Bad choices do not make you a bad person. It's such an important concept. I'll repeat it. *Bad choices do not make you a bad person.* They don't limit you either, without your permission to do so. You can change direction and make a new choice at any time. Of course, we have to acknowledge that some bad choices can have severe consequences. However, no matter what choice was made or where it has led us, we can pivot and head in another direction, literally at any moment. It is up to us!

When we decide to forgive ourselves and let go of our "bad choices," our new choices must be made from awareness, from clarity of purpose and intention. They must be conscious choices. Made from awareness of our thoughts, feelings, needs, wants, desires, passions, purpose, and learning. Awareness is a tool we must commit to using to make better decisions, better choices.

Reflection: **Let's reflect on a choice that you have made in your life. It can be yesterday, or it can be a decade ago. What steps did you take in making that choice? What was your motivation for making it? Did you make it out of fear? Did you make it because you wanted to please someone else? Did you make it because you were afraid of what people would think if you made a different choice? Was it made from a place of anger or to prove a point? Was it made because it seemed like the simpler path? It's important to be honest with yourself, but without judgment of yourself. Yes, without judgment. Judgment creates shame, embarrassment, and an inability to move forward. So, when you let go of the judgment and can be honest with yourself, real growth occurs. Yes, easier said than done, but I urge you to be open to the possibility of non-judgment as we go through the exercises in this book.**

Let's look at *choices* through a clarifying lens.

Identify a choice you've made and ask yourself: What if you had considered this choice from a state of awareness? What if you had made this choice considering your passion, purpose, values, needs, wants, desires? What if you had made this decision from a place of clarity and peace; self-love and reflection? Would the choice have been different? Write your thoughts below.

_____

_____

_____

_____

_____

_____

_____

_____

If the answer is yes, that is progress! Just a little introspection on a past event has created some self-awareness. We can't change the past, but we can change the course of our future.

When we make decisions and choices from a place of deep awareness, the outcomes are different. Choices are made that *serve* us. Because of our self-awareness, we can make decisions that serve our purpose, intention, passion, and values. We can learn to follow our intuition, and to listen to our "gut." This doesn't mean that the choices we make in awareness are the easy choices. Sometimes they are the hardest choices, but they are the ones we need to make to be aligned with our true purpose.

Truth Alert: **When reflecting, we must be *gentle* with ourselves. Coming to terms with some of our choice motivations is difficult. We know what the outcomes are, we're living them, but it doesn't make looking back any less stressful. The purpose of reviewing our decisions is not to shame us. We can't use our awareness as an excuse to berate ourselves. Instead, it should be a joyous realization that starting now, we can, in awareness, consciously create what's next. This is great news! When we know better, we do better (hopefully). It's time to do better.**

Becoming self-aware, and aware in general, starts with noticing the little things, the everyday things. It is a habit, a choice. It can be as simple as consciously feeling the warmth of the sun on our faces; or noticing how a tree sways in the wind; or the sounds of the birds in the morning; or the car horns in the city. Don't take these noises for granted because you are used to hearing them. Stop and listen. What exactly is going on around you? It's a symphony of sound or the harmony of white noise. Become aware of it. What do you notice?

_____

_____

_____

_____

_____

_____

_____

Let's do an exercise. You don't have to move. Just keep reading…

AWARENESS EXERCISE

Start with awareness of *now*. Take a deep breath. Feel the breath filling your lungs. Let it out through your nose. S-l-o-w-l-y. Feel air flowing out of your nose. Are you stuffy or is your nose clear? Does it feel good to take a deep breath or does it feel weird, heavy? Does it make you lightheaded?

Now, take another breath and as you become aware of your surroundings —as if for the first time. Really, through open eyes, look around and feel. What is the temperature of the room? Are you warm, comfortable, cold? Don't judge it, by getting engaged in the thought, instead just notice it.

Next, feel your "self". How are your neck, your back, shoulders, and legs feeling? Are they relaxed? Are they tense? Just notice. Are you slouching? Are you seated comfortably? Feel the chair or bed or couch, whatever is supporting your body. Is it hard or soft? Warm or cold? Just notice.

Now, listen. Deeply listen to the sounds around you. What do you hear? Take your time…no need to rush. You have nowhere to be. Just allow.

What do you hear? Do you hear the sound of children playing? Do you hear the sounds of other members of your family in the house? Or do you hear silence? Do you notice a clock ticking or the sounds of technology? Do you recognize the sound of the air conditioner or heater kicking on and off? Dogs barking? Again, no judgment of the sound (I know…easier said than done.) Just notice it. This is the beginning of awareness.

Now let's take another deep breath. A big, deep breath. This time let it out very, very, very slowly. Take a couple deeper breaths in the same manner. These are cleansing breaths.

And, notice your thoughts. What is going on in your internal dialogue? Are your thoughts incessant? Or have they silenced a bit? Become aware of what you are thinking and how those thoughts are creating your reality. Are they reminding you of all the things you need to do, but aren't doing? Are they supporting you in this moment? *Or* not? Are your thoughts silent?

Remember, just notice…and allow thoughts to exist. Try not to engage. But, if you do, don't judge it. Just take another breath and simply go back to concentrating on your breath.

Now take a step inside of yourself. Close your eyes. Imagine you are looking at yourself from the inside. Start at the top of your head. Keep scanning downward. Check in with your body. How is the top of your head? Is it clear, foggy, headachy? Just notice. How is your jaw? Is it clenched or relaxed? How about your shoulders? Do you need to release them? Travel down a bit further. Can you notice and feel your heartbeat? Put your attention and focus on your heart, specifically on the organ's pumping movement and beat. Don't think about it. Just notice it. What do you feel? What do you notice? If nothing, that's okay too!

Next, move to your gut…that area right in between your ribs, just below your chest. How does it feel? Is it tight? Anxious? Relaxed? Calm? Just notice. This is an area to pay very close attention to—it gives us great insight into what we are feeling and sensing. Our gut is an instrument I would highly recommend paying attention to and trusting.

This is just one exercise that can bring you to the state of *awareness*. And, in awareness, we can make changes. We can make a new choice, or step back when needed. Awareness opens our life, our heart, and our minds to great possibilities!

And, this, my friend, is just the beginning!

AWARENESS JOURNAL EXERCISE

My most significant shifts have come from discovering presence and being hyper-aware in any given moment. Awareness, however, is a learned skill, that comes from practice—and I'm still practicing. We all have those moments that we still remember so vividly. We can go back to that moment and remember how it felt—the colors, the smells, the energy, every movement. That was a moment of presence. And your awareness, in that moment, was a result of being present.

This exercise helps to develop the practice of awareness—of being present to your "self" and the world around you. There are many ways to get here — meditation, meditative walking, yoga, journaling, walking on the beach—or any other activity that brings you to clarity, your center, or a sense of peace.

The purpose of Awareness journaling is that the specific act of *becoming aware of your thoughts* trains the mind into the act of awareness of thought. This becomes a practice and will help you to shift into awareness at any given moment of your choosing. The insight you gain will help you greatly on this journey as we discover what is holding us back from our dreams.

Truth Alert: **This may bring up judgment and self-doubt. Allow it to be there, notice it, journal it, then let it go. The awareness of these feelings are key to a deeper sense of your beliefs. Remember, in awareness, we can choose to hang on tight, to let go, or to revisit it later. But, at least you have a choice. Are you ready?**

Awareness Journal Process

Get a journal—maybe a small one to keep with you as you start this process.

Use one page for each moment where you are journaling.

Break down the page into **Moment, Feelings, Thoughts, Outcome.** We've included a few pages for you to follow so you can start now. In any moment that it occurs to you, write down your thoughts and become aware of them and your reaction to them.

- Feel what is happening in your gut, how does it feel?
- What are your thoughts telling you?
- Are they questioning something or someone?
- Are they telling you what an idiot you are or are they open, loving, and forgiving?
- What are these thoughts telling you—what "beliefs" are showing up? Are they *limiting* beliefs? Do they serve you positively or negatively?
- What was the outcome of this moment? Did it end well? Did it end as expected? Or did it end better or worse?
- How did your thoughts create the outcome of the moment? Where can this awareness lead to a new thought or a shift in a belief?

Use the sheets that follow to note your answers to these questions.

Moment	Feelings	Thoughts	Outcome

Moment	Feelings	Thoughts	Outcome

Previously, I asked if your thoughts and beliefs serve you in a positive or negative way. You may be wondering how a thought that is negative can "serve you". What I learned years ago is that we sometimes get so comfortable in dysfunction that it becomes more justifiable and comfortable than peace and happiness.

That the dysfunction somehow serves (and justifies) our "story" and our life (albeit in an unhealthy way). You push back and say, "Why would I do anything, which negatively serves me?" and my answer is that it is more comfortable than the shift in thinking, believing and judgment necessary to recognize the dysfunction and make a new choice. We get invested in "and even defensive" of our way of living and thinking.

We are oftentimes fearful of the other side of the only way we've ever known. Understandable. The question then becomes, what are you willing to do to change those beliefs, thoughts, behaviors. If your answer is "I deeply want something different. I'm ready to walk through the fire. Then it is time, let's go!

If you are not ready, that's okay too. Just acknowledge where you are and keep journaling. Be open to what shows up and please know that the life you want is there for the taking—when you are ready to take it. In the meantime, be gentle with yourself and keep reading.

VOICES IN YOUR HEAD EXERCISE

The awareness journal exercise helps you to practice being "aware" in a moment. To recognize how your body and thoughts are contributing to the moment you are in. To be in awareness of your feelings, beliefs, and actions and how they result in behaviors, words, and outcomes.

This awareness exercise will also contribute to the practice of awareness; however, this one focuses solely on the thoughts in our head at any given time—whether you are walking a dog, running on the treadmill, or eating dinner. Some stats say we have over 80,000 thoughts a day. Yes, 80,000. How many of those thoughts are you aware? And, if you are not aware of them, how often are the thoughts driving your life instead of you consciously driving your life based on your dreams; your desired outcomes?

This exercise will help to shed light on the unconscious thoughts creating the world we *see*.

Activity:

1. Create "awareness" of the voices in your head—the constant conversation and communication that is going on internally. It is incessant. We have thousands of thoughts per day, only a few of which serve us.

2. Journal the voices in your head—the lies we tell ourselves (Examples: "I'm not good enough." "I'm not pretty enough." "I'm not smart enough." "I've got this." "Who do they think they are?" "My mom was right." And on and on they go. Keep writing. Don't go back and review. Don't cross anything out. Don't try to make the sentences perfect. Just write. As you are aware…write. Write what is happening around you…and your reaction to it.

3. Write what is going through your head. Do this when you are happy. Do this when you are angry. Do this when you are just working at your desk or stressed, and a thought pops into your head. Just write.

4. Don't judge the thoughts. Don't make them wrong, right, bad or good. Just notice they are there. Why is this important? Because in awareness, we can shift our thoughts, feelings, and reactions. In awareness, we can change anything, if we choose to.

THE THOUGHTS IN MY HEAD

Date:	Environment:

Thoughts

Date:	Environment:

Thoughts:

Journaling is a tool to begin to create the awareness.

Awareness brings the darkness to the light. It shines a flashlight on those thoughts that are driving your behaviors. And, anything that is brought to the light doesn't have a chance of survival—unless we allow it life. This is when the real work begins.

CHAPTER 3:

THE STORY YOU TELL

> *The whole story is about you. You are the main character.*
>
> *—Don Miguel Ruiz*

Understanding your story will help you to understand why your life is your life today. Your story informs and determines your actual view of the world around you.

Through self-reflection and growth, I have learned that it is not our life that informs or defines our story. Instead, it is *our story* that informs and determines our life. If your life is not as you desire, you must start by rewriting your story. The first step is to understand the story you've been telling yourself, and others, all these years.

So, what exactly is "your story"? It's the story you tell when someone asks about you. It may be a simple story or an elaborate one, but mostly it's a tale bursting with untruths cloaked as absolute truth. It may be built from the lies we tell ourselves. Lies like, "I'm not good enough." "They don't like me because…" "I messed up so I will never get anywhere." "I'll never get what I want." "I was born a loser, and I will always be a loser." "I am who I am." "I don't deserve anything more." "I am not pretty enough." "I am not thin enough." "I am not rich enough." "I'm just unlucky." "I am not worthy of (insert your favorite limiting belief/lie here)."

As you can imagine, by the power of these words, your story matters. Those untruths (beliefs) can take on lives of their own. Your story has energy and it has meaning. It matters both how you tell your story, and how you live it. It matters because it is full of your experiences, perceived through the filters of a lifetime of stories, beliefs, and society's tales. Your story expands and grows depending on how much emotion is attached to it.

Most likely, your story is an unconscious creation—created over years of living and through other people's stories. It is a result of pain, joy, disappointment, love, anger, courage, and more. Your story is derived from your perception of the experiences, and the information you received from the world around you. It is a complex story weaved through a lifetime, affecting all the cells of your being.

The good news is that your story, when understood from a place of awareness and consciousness, provides insight and guidance for change, and potentially creates a new story, consciously. In your willingness to create a new story or re-tool the old one, change can be made.

Note: As you become aware of your story's energy and power, you may find a willingness to rewrite your story *now, today*. Be patient. We will get there!

These exercises will help to ensure your new story; your new beginning is conscious, truthful and inspiring.

Right now, however, your story might not be any of those things (conscious, truthful or inspiring). Right now, it might be a less than powerful mix of lies and limiting beliefs. It might be peppered with fear-based platitudes like, "I can't because it's too hard." "They will laugh at me." "I am not smart enough." "I haven't had the benefit of those advantages." "I'm starting from nothing. I don't stand a chance."

Your story is born of your past. It was given life by a few impactful experiences that led to blanket perceptions of how the world works. It came from something someone once said to you, or something that happened to you, to which you assigned particular significance. It came from your judgments of what is "good," "bad," "valuable," or "beautiful." It came from comparing yourself to others or being compared to others by important people in your life. Maybe a parent or teacher (dealing with their own story!) said, "You can't do that." "You are not smart enough." "You aren't capable." "Who do you think you are?" "People like us can only go so far in life." Those experiences and *their* words became *your* beliefs. They became your truth! You internalized them to the point where you actually believed them, and they have colored and defined every experience since. They are the glasses through which you see the world. Unfortunately, these beliefs have become your truth, and they are laden with fear, self-doubt, shame, and judgment.

Your story begins to act as a fortune-teller, and it carries the power and energy to create the world you see.

Think about a time when someone asked you, "Hey when you get a minute, I need to talk to you about something." Immediately your story (the story you tell yourself in your own head) helps predict the future and it's never good.

The story we create in our head goes something like this: "I'm going to get fired." "I did something wrong." "He/she is going to break up with me." "Why does this always happen to me." We play out the scene (that has not yet occurred) and various (negative) scenarios without even knowing the subject of the conversation. Every insecurity, self-doubt, fear, and story from the last "conversation" someone requested to have with us plays out. You end up living through a Shakespearean tragedy before anything actually occurs. Imagine how draining that is for your psyche, and how detrimental that is to your well-being.

And, further, since thoughts are energy, imagine what you are unconsciously creating when the truth can be as simple as a request for you to take on a new project or an idea for a vacation!

My Financial Belief Story

When I was seven or eight, I remember vividly wanting to go the movies one day in the summer. My mom called the movie theater to ask if they accepted checks. This was the 70s and people still paid by check! She put the phone down and turned to us and quietly said, "No." The movie theater didn't accept checks. My heart sank. But not for the reason you think. It wasn't because I couldn't go to the movies. It was because I could see the truth on my mom's face. I knew they accepted checks. Somehow, I understood we had no money. I saw her hurt, her disappointment. I could feel her pain. She couldn't even take her kids to the movies on a summer day. I could feel her desperation.

I know that at that very moment, her struggle became mine. My story had a new component. My belief that money was difficult to come by was born. It was my family's story, and it became mine.

My struggle with money continued for a long time. I always made money, but I worked very hard for it. I worked two jobs throughout college to pay my tuition, my apartment, and all my bills because I didn't want any debt. But, of course, I wanted more stuff, so I took on debt. I had everything I wanted, but couldn't afford it, so I took on debt to have those things. It was terrifying. It took many, many years, and a lot of internal work and dialog to begin rewriting my financial belief story.

But, first, I had to understand it, as well as all of the other experiences that formed my story. I had to look into the mirror. I had to let go of *their* story to create *my own*. I had to forgive and to let go of the judgments I had around my upbringing, my family, and money. I had to be willing to own the life I had created and re-write my story to include the life I wanted to live and the story I wanted to tell. And, I learned, along the way, that we have multiple experiences that contribute to our overall story and it is how we see and how we incorporate those experiences into our truth, and how those truths become our beliefs, which define our story.

STORY EXERCISE

What is your story? This may be difficult and painful when you first start to write. Below you'll find some prompts. You can use them to get started, or you can begin putting your story on paper whichever you prefer.

Write down the stories you tell yourself with awareness, brutal honesty and openness to change. How will I do this, you ask? How do I know what stories I tell myself versus what is true for me? The stories and the truth have become one, so don't use logic in this exercise, just write.

Don't "adjust" it to make yourself the hero or to defend your story. Instead, be brutally honest and fact-based with your story.

Chances are, they are all stories you tell yourself. Only in complete awareness, acceptance, and lack of judgment does truth exist—i.e., no story. So, write them down. Write down the story you tell others about your life. Write down the story you tell yourself about the reasons your life exists as it does today. Don't judge them as truth or lies, as good or bad, as worthy or unworthy. Otherwise, you will only write down what you believe is "bad," when sometimes what you judge is "good" isn't serving you either. Just write them down. No censoring. No judgment.

Faithfully start keeping a journal—start with this book. Keep track of what is going on in your head when you are stopping yourself, when you are worrying, when you are fearful, and when you are angry. Keep track of what you are telling yourself when you are happy, or when you have landed the client you've always wanted, when you are meeting with your boss or an employee, after the meeting, etc. There is clarity in all the stories.

To truly change, there must be a *willingness* to change. A willingness to "see" and a desire to shift. There will be a lot of emotion around this exercise. Just go with it. Do not stop yourself from feeling the emotions that come up or from changing the story in that moment, because you judge it negatively. Part of being able to let go of and change our story is the ability to walk through it and allow it to exist as it is, not wishing for it to be different or resenting it for being the way it is. It requires feeling where you are deep down and appreciating it as part of who you are today. Be grateful for the learning, the experiences, the necessary part of your path up to this moment—it got you here, thinking differently, seeking more; moving towards the life you want to live. When you feel, understand and recognize that the story isn't serving you and you desire something different, you'll be able to shift toward what will be your *new* story and your new *truth*.

NOTE: It is imperative *not* to judge your story. Many of my coaching clients ask, "How do I know if I'm judging?" Chances are strong that you are judging. "Ugh. My story sucks. I'm a mess." That is judging. "My life is boring. Not much of a story here." That is judging. "Wow! My life isn't that bad. I'm awesome." That too is judging!!

Defining your story as good, bad, a mess, acceptable, boring, unacceptable, awesome, or any other adjective, comes from judgment. It is, however, what we do and have always done. So, when you say to yourself, "Oh my goodness, everything I do is judging." Just laugh and, well, don't judge it!

Here are some questions/prompts to get you started. These are the everyday questions that someone may ask you:

START WITH WHAT YOU KNOW AND BUILD FROM THERE

---

1. What do you tell people when they ask about your childhood? How was your childhood? Chaotic? Loving? Dysfunctional? Angry? Fun?

_____

_____

_____

_____

_____

2. How did your life unfold from childhood to where you are today? What is the story you tell there?

_____

_____

_____

_____

_____

3. What is your response when people ask about your education or experience?

_____

_____

_____

_____

_____

_____

4. What is the story you tell about how you met your significant other? Or about your divorce? Or about being single or being married?

_____

_____

_____

_____

_____

_____

5. What is the story you tell when others ask about your schoolwork or your job?

_____

_____

_____

_____

_____

6. How do you describe your parents out loud? How do you describe them to yourself? Is it different?

_____

_____

_____

_____

_____

_____

7. Where did you grow up? What meaning does that have to your story?

_____

_____

_____

_____

_____

_____

8. Describe your parents. Do you have siblings? Are they in the story or excluded?

_____

_____

_____

_____

_____

_____

9. What is your profession? How do you define yourself? Are you a stay-at-home-mom? An executive? A business owner? A woman business owner? A student? Unemployed? What do you answer when someone asks you, "What do you do?"

_____

_____

_____

_____

_____

_____

10. Are you successful? What is the story you tell about your success?

_____

_____

_____

_____

_____

11. How are your finances? Abundant? Lacking? Why?

_____

_____

_____

_____

_____

_____

12. Why is your life not as you desire? Write the story you tell yourself and others.

_____

_____

_____

_____

_____

_____

13. How has your story changed through the years?

_____

_____

_____

_____

_____

_____

_____

_____

_____

_____

_____

_____

Other insights into the story you tell.

_____

_____

_____

_____

_____

_____

_____

_____

_____

_____

_____

_____

_____

I've answered the questions, now what do I do?

Remember, the reason for this exercise is to gain awareness. So let's get some insight into our "selves" and our story. Be aware of your thoughts and feelings as you read the following and refer back to your story. Notice the emotion, defensiveness, pride, judgment, shame, or any other feelings that come up. Just notice…

How does the city you grew up in matter to your story? Is it written in passing or is it meaningful because of the city's name, its history, culture, etc.?

_____

_____

_____

_____

_____

Notice the truth of your upbringing. What words did you use to describe your childhood? How do those words affect you? Are there strong emotions in this section or not?

_____

_____

_____

_____

_____

How about your profession or status in life? Did you define it or did it define you? Did you choose your path because someone told you what you should be or do? Did circumstances limit you? Did you hold yourself back? Did you overcome significant obstacles in the process? What is that story? Is it written? Is it something you tell yourself and others?

_____

_____

_____

_____

_____

How much judgment is present in your story? Are there untruths in your story to cover a truth of which you are ashamed, or you believe will be judged by others? Just notice. Don't judge.

_____

_____

_____

_____

_____

Look at places in your story where you feel defensive, emotional, angry, embarrassed, proud, frustrated, sad, or happy. And, look at your belief about "why" that feeling exists. Acknowledge those here.

_____

_____

_____

_____

_____

_____

What is the Mindset in this story? What Beliefs exist in this story to allow it to be a *true* story?

Why did I ask these questions? Why did I ask you to notice?

The reason is because through *awareness first* and *action second*, you can affect change. You can even write a new story. Awareness of the old story and an understanding of how it has created your life as it is today will spark the insight (and fire) to write your NEW story. This story will come from consciousness, purpose, passion, and your definition of an ideal life.

_____

The Business Perspective: A Client's Story

Her story starts with the following statement: "I can't move up because all the big deals go to Matt." And continues with:

Management likes Matt because he has a bigger book of business since he has been here longer. Since all the deals go to him, his experience is better represented in the community. The market knows and respects him, so even the market goes to him first. And, on top of that, this is such a competitive market that every time I meet with a friend or prospect, they tell me they already have a financial advisor. I'm spinning my wheels.

On the other hand, Matt has so much work to do always. He doesn't even leave his desk. The phone rings off the hook for him. So, I have to work harder. I have to be out of the office more meeting people and hoping for a lead. In the end, everyone defers to Matt, and I get the scraps.

So, what do you think the outcome was? Yep, you guessed it. She got everything she expected, making less money and struggling, just as her story described. Fewer deals that she had to really work hard to land. The truth is, she was probably energetically building Matt's business through her belief that Matt was so successful there was no point in trying to compete. Everything her story told came true. Her story was a self-fulfilling prophecy.

And our stories are too!

So, what would happen if she changed her view? Her view would change! As Wayne Dyer once quoted: "When you change the way you look at things, the things you look at change."

What you see, what you believe, what you state, you will create. Period.

Truth Alert: **It's never as simple as just changing your thoughts. When your thoughts don't align with your beliefs, your words hold no power of change. So, just using "Positive Thought" on its own, without changing your deeply held beliefs won't do enough. You must change both.**

This was my response to my client:

Maybe Matt is fantastic and is the best salesperson around. Maybe your story is true. It is certainly true to you. Most likely, it is a fabrication, created by your limiting beliefs, fears and stories. However, I can assure you that as long as this is your story—the story you tell your friends, the story you tell yourself, the story you tell your colleagues—the world will continue to conspire to make it true.

Remember that your story, whether it is true or not, is energy. Energy creates like energy. So, you are giving away all your power (and responsibility for your success), by believing and repeating this self-limiting story and not owning the results.

Because of the intense energy of "lack" and "blame," your innate power and truth cannot be seen or heard by you, your colleagues, or the marketplace. You are always working and responding from your story of "lack" and "blame" and your underlying beliefs of "not good enough" and "woe is me."

However, *awareness* is critical. The minute you become aware that the story is a fictional representation of what is happening around you, most likely made up by ego and fear, that is the moment you can change the story if you choose. Only in awareness, can real change come.

So…how do we get out of our lies and into our Truth? How do we tell a new story that serves us? That opens us to the truth of our soul and our deeper purpose?

Let's start with our beliefs…

CHAPTER 4:

YOUR BELIEFS DEFINE THE WORLD YOU SEE

> *Your beliefs become your thoughts. Your thoughts become your words. Your words become your actions. Your actions become your habits. Your habits become your values. Your values become your destiny.*
>
> —*Mahatma Ghandi*

Think about that—our beliefs define the world we see. So, if we believe life is a struggle, we will experience and see examples all around us of struggle. If we believe life is beautiful and exciting, then that is how the world will show up for us.

Where it gets tricky is in understanding what we *really* believe. Understanding the unconscious, always present, thoughts, beliefs and judgments operating in the background, in the dark, driving our actions.

We may think that we believe "it is what it is" and that we are in acceptance of everything happening just as it should. However, is that *really* what you believe? Or is it something you tell yourself while resisting the *acceptance* of this moment.

Or, do you think you believe that everything is easy, but it shows up as a struggle?

To understand our beliefs entirely, we must look further, and deeper.

INSIGHT EXERCISE

Read your story as you wrote it above. Next, re-read your story, from the perspective of what is showing up as a belief, even if you didn't write it as "I believe that..." Usually, our beliefs aren't easily discovered. Our beliefs are deeply rooted and frequently show up as absolute truth.

Statements like: "Life hasn't been easy." Or "My parents really messed up my life." Or "Money was always a struggle." These are your beliefs although you may have *great* evidence to back up your statement as fact and the "scars" to prove it. What did you discover? Write it here.

Underlying beliefs showing up in my story:

_____

_____

_____

_____

_____

_____

_____

_____

_____

_____

_____

_____

_____

_____

_____

_____

_____

   Think about it. Our experiences, may unconsciously, create our beliefs. We respond, act, choose, and live based on these beliefs. And, these beliefs continue to create (yes, *create*) the life we live. It is a vicious cycle.

   A great example of how our underlying beliefs create the world we see is when five people are witness to a single event. It can be a wonderful, or a tragic, event. But, chances are, of the 5, all or many will have very different stories of *what* they saw, and many will even "make up" the *why* the event happened—creating their (our) own story, their (our) own truth and view of the event. However, it becomes their (our) truth, based on their (our) beliefs, and their (our) experiences.

In our life *our* truth is *our* truth, and *their* truth is *their* truth.

We immediately believe *our* truth, created from our view, over someone else's truth, created from their view. And, vice versa.

So, whose truth is the right truth in this situation? Whose story is correct? Whose truth should be told? Are my beliefs, my experiences, my truths any less valid than someone else's? Are theirs any less valid than mine?

This book is about you and how you relate to the world. So, a better question is this: How much of what I saw is actual, factual, non-emotional truth and not colored by my deeply held beliefs, my unconscious desire, my need for control, my judgments, my story or my need to be heard? How much of what you witnessed was from awareness and presence in that moment?

Hopefully, this brings you, my precious reader, to the question of: "Oh my! How much of what I see comes from my unconscious beliefs and how much of what I see comes from present-moment awareness?" And, how does all this affect my story and the life I lead? Read on…

———————————————

Beliefs, Thoughts, Action

Before we can move on to creating our life our way, we must better understand and acknowledge the underlying path to our actions, reactions, and behaviors. We must first use what you have learned and are learning through awareness.

And, here's why:

- Our experiences create our beliefs.

- Our beliefs create our thoughts.

- Our thoughts create our actions and reactions.

It's a vicious cycle and it is mostly unconscious. Some of our beliefs are created as infants. That is why we are told, as parents, that our children learn "trust" by the age of 2. Whether they are fed, changed, nurtured, and loved matters. It determines whether a bond is formed and how they respond to the world! And, that continues all throughout our life. Every experience plants a seed. So, imagine how your memories and experiences may be creating your beliefs about yourself and the world today.

INSIGHT EXERCISE

Think about your life for a moment. Think about some of your happiest moments. Those moments when you were laughing with your friends, your family. A moment when you received some great news. A moment you felt at peace, safe, and in-flow. A time when everything was just right, and you didn't want the moment to end.

Okay…do you remember it? Can you remember the emotion of it?

How did you feel?

What did you "learn" in that moment?

Did you learn that someone loved you?

Did you learn that you were capable of anything?

Did you learn that your life was going to change brilliantly?

What did that moment teach you?

_____

_____

_____

_____

_____

_____

_____

Moment	Feelings	Outcome	Learning	Belief

In other words, what "belief" was born out of that moment or those times in your life? What did you incorporate into your arsenal of truth, that now drives what you believe and how you react to the world?

Does that "truth" or belief still exist for you today? Or has some other experience, maybe not as great, changed your thoughts about that moment?

I created this first exercise from the positive even though, at times, it's easier to find an unhappy memory or experience. We can and must learn from both.

Now, think of an unhappy moment or time. Really think about it. Feel it. What were you thinking at the time? What are you thinking now? Write it down.

_____

_____

_____

_____

_____

_____

_____

_____

_____

_____

These are the beliefs that were, and may still be, being actively created. Experience is one of the avenues that create our beliefs, unconsciously. What part of the experience creates the belief? The judgment of the experience is what creates the belief. And, the judgment comes from either your "learning" or someone else's teaching, which came from their beliefs, born out of their judgments. Exhausting!

How Do Someone Else's Beliefs Become Ours?

What often happens is the *outside world* defines our truth for us! We allow "their" fears, beliefs, experiences to inform the world we see. Remember, we always have a choice. Those choices begin to serve our life, our success, as we learn to guide ourselves from the inside-out. This is where pure change can happen from our soul's truth.

Unfortunately, society, and often our families, have taught us to live from the outside-in. That is where our fight for our lives begins. Learning to listen to our "self" is where we can begin to transition to our God-given power.

The Choices in Our Stories

Let's take a real-world example. How does "prejudice" exist?

In my earlier story, I mentioned growing up in a home where prejudice was taught through example. It was the way (many, not all) spoke about others based on their religion, the color of their skin, their language, how they looked, or even their weight! The adults in our home did not discriminate on how they would discriminate - when it came to prejudice! And, being female was also "less than"—so there were different rules and different treatment, based on gender. There were no limits of judgment in our home.

Thankfully, somehow, as a young child, I sensed and even rebelled against what I *knew* (my truth) was an injustice. My gut said this is wrong and I resisted their beliefs, their negative words; and I fought for "their" words to not become my own. I was often bullied by my family, as a result. The adults in my family would joke that I was adopted and, I hoped I was. My mom, however, was a light on this path. She supported my independent thought and explained two things:

1. Their prejudices were a result of their upbringing and what they had seen, experienced and been taught, which didn't make it right, but was so. She further explained that their reaction to others was most likely born out of fear of not being good enough! And, although I had to respect them as my elders, I did not need to believe in the same way they did, nor speak or act in the same way.

2. And, second, that I was no better than anyone else. And, no worse. She further explained that we are all going through something all the time and how I saw the world was up to me (as it was up to them). That we each had a choice.

Although there was love and support in our home, it was a lot to overcome as a child. Their beliefs and actions did, unfortunately, limit my thoughts; determined who I could bring home; and at times limited what I could say and how I could express myself, so there was always tension in our home. However, as I got older, I kept quiet less and less, allowing my beliefs to be expressed, which added tension to a home already walking a tightrope of dysfunction and pain.

Over time, and after releasing much anger and hurt, I realized (and came to believe) that I had a choice, and that judgment of myself and others came from me—not from what I was taught. I understood right from wrong, which was also taught. And as I began to think for myself, to learn and to grow, I understood that my beliefs, my way of being, was a choice.

You see, I could have chosen to believe that I was better or different, because of the color of my skin, or my religion, or the language I spoke or the country I was born in, or because I was female—because that is what my family tried to teach me. I could have continued to learn from them, ignoring my truth, and become a parrot of their teaching, their beliefs, their choices.

Or I could choose my own path. I could choose to believe that we are all the same, forging life's path, and although those paths may be different, we are all still the same. We are all human beings trying to figure this life out. There are probably a million other beliefs in between, but the understanding that choice was and is always mine, became my superpower, to live my life my way. I can't change another living being, but I can change me.

EXERCISE

As our beliefs become our truths, and those beliefs and truths define the world around us, bringing those beliefs to the light is important to finding the truth we require.

What are the beliefs you have that have been handed down to you? Societal beliefs? Rules you "must" follow? Family beliefs?

Write them down. Ask yourself: Do your beliefs serve you? Are they creating the life you *want* to lead? The story you *desire* to tell?

SECTION 2

WRITING THE STORY YOU WISH TO TELL

To write our new story, the story which will inform the life we live, we must be in touch with our truth. Our truth is derived from our greater purpose. Our purpose, once uncovered, is our guiding light. It reminds us of why we are willing to work hard and take intentional, meaningful action. Our plan gives us direction and focus to ensure we are taking the *right* action. Taking the *right action* will ensure our story unfolds in alignment with our purpose.

CHAPTER 5:

GETTING TO SHEDEFINING YOUR STORY:
CREATING CONSCIOUS BELIEFS

> *As you commence the next stage of your life, you can follow someone else's script, try to make choices that will make other people happy, avoid discomfort, do what is expected, and copy the status quo. Or you can look at all that you have accomplished today and use it as fuel to venture forth and write your own story. If you do, amazing things will take shape.*
>
> —Kerry Washington

Awareness and Insight

This is where the exercises in this book and your Awareness Journaling, hopefully, bring about insight. Specifically, awareness of the stories we tell the world and ourselves brings insight into where the story came from. This will guide us to writing the story we want to tell; the story of the unfolding of our dream life, our success in business, our success as a parent, our meaning as a human being .

"Why," you ask. Why does this insight provide the ability to change the story? Because *at the moment of awareness, you can make a different choice, if you choose to.* You can search for a deeper sense of truth and power. You can allow, learn, forgive, and let go. Anything you bring to the light cannot exist in darkness. In the light, you can see it for what it is: good, bad, or ugly. In the dark, the beliefs, the thoughts continue to grow and expand as insidiously as mold grows. Awareness is the flashlight in the dark. You may not like what you see at first; however, once you see "it", you can decide to keep it or change it.

In the light, in awareness, you have the power of choice.

But as long as it remains in the dark, in the shadows, in your fake truth, it flourishes, and your power to change is diminished by the darkness

Let's look at another scenario:

Often our story incorporates that which we believe we have no control over. I often hear stories like: "My home life is chaotic." "I have no peace." "My husband and I can't even discuss simple things anymore without fighting." Those are experiences that have become your beliefs, creating more of the same.

For business owners, I often hear:

"I can't move forward without funding." "I don't have the right customers." "I am spinning my wheels, and nothing changes." "There is not enough time to do it all." "I can't do this anymore."

How much of those thoughts and words are beliefs? How do these words inform their reality? Do you think the thoughts, beliefs, words, and actions of someone who succeeds are different than those above?

Now, think deeper. How do your thoughts, beliefs, words, and actions move you closer to or further away from the life you want to lead?

How does your story inform your reality?

Does this story empower or disempower?

Does it serve your peace or destroy it?

Remember, the stories we tell inform the truth of our experience.

How about this story. It is just two sentences

"Everyone is fighting, and I'm stuck in the middle, trying to make it work. I really can't take it anymore. "

What makes you "stuck" in the middle? Explore the choices and beliefs that have put you in the middle *and* are preventing you from getting out? What new story could be told?

What if the "story" that was told in this family was—"We have had our battles, but we are learning to talk through our differences. We may not always see eye-to-eye, but we accept that each has their own opinion and truth and just because it is different from mine, doesn't make them wrong. I don't get in the middle of someone else's fight, because it serves no one. Instead, we've discussed this as a family, and we will only support open communication and healthy conflict but will no longer support rudeness and disrespect. I find my own peace and allow others to find theirs. We are learning and growing through this process."

"But, how?" you ask. How do you get to this story? Well, without this new story (or by holding tightly onto the old story), you can never get to peace. This story allows you to figure out what needs to be done to get to this story. It helps us to determine what boundaries need to be set; what learning and inner work you must do to find your way to removing yourself from the middle (a choice that is being made).

Truth Alert: **Gaining clarity and awareness of what thoughts, beliefs, and actions created the old story, and your role in it, allows for the choice to change the story and to let go of old habits, beliefs, fears, and behaviors that allowed the old story to exist and to write the new story.**

Never forget (or please remind yourself) that you have *everything* you need inside of you to create the life of your dreams. You've created your life up to this point. You've just created it unconsciously, from your untruths, and without purpose, so you took a little detour. No judgment. There is so much learning on this path.

The learning, however, is that you (and only you) hold the key. You possess the truth within you. And, from awareness you "get to" create a life of conscious choice based on your passion and purpose.

This is why the assignments and exercises in this book are so important. This is why writing down and understanding your story is so very necessary. Because until you are aware, you cannot shift that which is driving your truth.

WRITING YOUR NEW STORY EXERCISE

These exercises have brought you awareness and insight into how you have gotten here in your life. If you have a new vision of your life or your business, it's time to get clarity on that. However, it would be great to take your old story and redefine or reframe it. This exercise brings learning to the process of how our story informs our life.

I'll lead by example of my new story as it relates to growing up. You remember the story of my upbringing. I've peppered the book with some of my insights from that upbringing, however, I do have a new truth of how I tell my story. Here it goes:

I was born into a home with lots of love. I was blessed to have a mom who showed me unconditional acceptance and love and through her lessons I was able to open my heart to acceptance and love.

I grew up in a home full of energy and fun. Our parents were hard-working and through that effort they often found ways to get 6 kids to Disney world or, when money was tight, they found free things to do, like take all of us to spend a day at the beach. I experienced their struggle and I saw their fight to succeed and move forward.

Through the love and imperfections in my family life, there was much learning, as is intended on our path. I learned much about the disease of addiction and how it affects us individually and as a society. This learning has opened my heart to a world of suffering and those in my family who continue to work to overcome this disease. It has taught me about acceptance and my ability to own the outcome. The lessons in addiction have taught me that we need to meet people where they are, not to come at them from where we are. These lessons have taught me to support others to make choices for their lives and that they (we individually) own the power to change our lives. The lessons of addiction have taught me kindness, compassion, and love for self and others.

Through the love and imperfections in my family life, I learned about prejudice, racism, and self-love. I learned about how our thoughts, our beliefs, our awareness creates the world we see. I learned there are a million different ways to "see" a situation and that I always have a choice in that view and my response to others' views. I learned to forgive, to allow, and to let go. I learned I get to choose my view and how I experience the world. I created a belief that we are all one in this world and as I do to myself I do to others. And as I do to others, I do to myself. I love that I have the power to choose love, to give love, and to receive love. And, I do it freely.

Through the love and imperfections in my family life, I learned how others' beliefs, thoughts, and actions can become our beliefs, thoughts, and actions. And, through years of pain and hurt, I discovered that I had a choice in it all. I learned the power of awareness, so that I can choose my own beliefs, thoughts, and actions. I have discovered a path of learning and continual growth. *I have discovered me.*

And, through the love and imperfections of my life, I have learned that there is no failure unless we quit – that there is learning or there is success. I've experienced the truth of the power of our thoughts and have learned that I possess the power to change and define my life, my way.

And, through the love and imperfections of my life, I have learned to judge less; love and forgive more. I have learned that my imperfections are perfect and in gratitude I have a fighting chance.

My story is that everything and everyone is here for a reason and that I get to choose *how* I see the world. My story is that I am grateful for the love and imperfection, the dysfunction and the pain, the joy and the learning, the never-ending opportunity to build the life of my choosing. And, that I'm not perfect and that is okay!

Now, it is your turn. What is the true story? What is the story you wish to tell the world? Tell it here. Write it as if it is happening today. Begin with: "My life is just as I had hoped…." Or "My business is hugely successful and the impact on the world is palpable…"

Think about it from our greatest dream; your greatest vision for your life. Dream big. Get into a quiet, focused space and write your new story:

_____

_____

_____

_____

_____

_____

_____

_____

_____

_____

_____

CHAPTER 6:

BUT FIRST, THE TRUTH:
LISTENING TO THE WHISPERS OF YOUR SOUL

> *What I know for sure is that you feel real joy in direct proportion to how connected you are to living your truth.*
>
> *—Oprah Winfrey*

The first step to SheDefining your story is discovering the *truth* of who we are and who we choose to be in this world.

For me, reality hit when I took the time to write my story of my business. I became aware of the tapes that ran and the story I told myself about my position in the market. At the time, I was in my 40s, recently divorced, and ready to take on the world. Well, sort of.

My Story

I was starting over in many respects. I was a single mom, starting a new company, recently divorced (my choice) and I had bills to pay. I wasn't financially struggling at that point, but my fears of financial struggle were about to hold me back in a huge way.

Part of my story was financial. Remember, I believed from childhood that money was a struggle.

My "beliefs" that:

- I have to take this gig at this rate because there is nothing else coming my way (fear)

Produced this:

- Low paying jobs (I set the hourly rate, don't forget) because I was fearful of "No, you're too expensive," which, by the way, created clients who said, "No, you're too expensive!"

The truth was, these clients did not understand my value because I did not understand my value and therefore I could not communicate my value. I ended up taking a "job" for a client to create steady income. Not my finest hour because I understood that fear was driving my choices instead of my innate power and *knowing* driving my choices.

When I eventually went back out on my own, I was determined to define my value *and* my truth. I remember one crucial encounter that did not resonate until I actually started to understand my story and my self-imposed limiting beliefs.

I was called into a manufacturing company with revenues around $35 million. They were moving from start-up to profitable rapidly. It was a great contract. They needed structure and a strong foundation to move forward. They were heading from "doing whatever it takes" to "getting the job done" towards "doing it right, because it matters." This is a make-it-or-break-it stage for many growing companies.

I had built a great rapport with the CEO and the executive team. It was a 6-9 month project, maybe 12 months. I was very excited and confident. I gave them a "great" project rate, and it was steady work that would still allow me to take on a couple of smaller companies.

The CEO called me to let me know they had awarded the contract to another firm—a firm from outside of the state! She said to me, "You didn't get the contract because your rates were too low." My head spun in confusion and disbelief. She continued, "You either didn't understand the scope, or you are at a lower level of consulting than the other companies that quoted."

"What?!" I thought to myself. How is this happening? At a lower level? What is she talking about? Who does she think she is?

"We all wanted you," she continued. "We all thought you would have a great impact on the company, on us individually, and as a team. We went with our number two. "Between you and I," she continued, " I suspect it is just that you don't know your value. When you figure that out, you will set the world on fire."

Wow. Wow. Wow. I put down the phone dumbfounded. Perception is *everything*. And *insight* changes everything.

Initially, I was angry. Then I was in victim mode. "That's what you get for trying to make it reasonable and make it a win-win," I thought. "They don't know what they are missing." My ego was on fire. And then, my tough thoughts melted into tears.

The words, "I suspect you don't know your value," kept repeating over and over again in my mind. Finally, my tears dried and I said to myself, "Holy crap. She's right." That was my turning point. That is where *this* journey began.

My story, not my truth, was holding me back. My aha moment was the awareness of that fact. My growth and change (my power) came from going inward, becoming aware and rewriting my story.

My unique value, my strengths, my gifts…that is my truth. I was born perfectly, with all that I need, to live a life of abundance, learning, love, forgiveness, peace, success and kindness. That is my story.

And, it started here, journaling to understand the truth of my ability, capability, power, self, and more. Acknowledging my power by defining my value, my purpose, my role in my success as a business owner and a person.

And now it is your turn to discover *your* truth.

DISCOVERING YOUR TRUTH ASSIGNMENT

Your truth begins with a deep exploration of self. This may be a completely new experience for you. Or not. Either way, this next exercise will take you step-by-step into exploring and discovering your deeper truth.

Step 1: Re-read your story. Is it still emotional? Read it again. Remember, it's a story. It's neither true nor untrue. It is just a story. The validity and power of that story come from your beliefs. For now, set it aside.

THE truth vs. YOUR truth

1. Write a list of your strengths, but not in comparison to others. Are you analytical, intuitive, good with people, reliable, logical, big picture, can execute on anything? Don't judge it as "bragging" or "arrogant." Instead, write it with an open and loving (of yourself) heart.

_____

_____

_____

_____

_____

_____

_____

_____

2. List your education, experience, and knowledge. Again, no judgments! Just write. This includes all experience and knowledge gained. Not just certificates or degrees. We gain most of our knowledge through experience. You are smarter and more experienced than you may believe!

_____

_____

_____

_____

_____

_____

_____

_____

_____

_____

_____

_____

_____

3. List your personal traits, such as: beautiful from the inside out, kind, open, honest, loving, want the best for everyone, hard-worker, love life, full of integrity, willing to be imperfect. Don't judge this. Just write. If you insist on defining what you are writing, then define these traits as the perfection bestowed on you at birth; the perfection in the imperfection. If this is difficult, list what it is that others say about you regarding your strengths. What are the compliments they give you?

_____

_____

_____

_____

_____

_____

_____

_____

_____

_____

_____

_____

4. Define what you don't necessarily enjoy doing but are doing nonetheless or need to do at the moment. To help you along—these are the tasks that you dread, put off, or feel anxious while you are doing them. These tasks are our procrastination triggers.

\

\

\

\

\

\

\

\

\

\

\

---

5. Next, define your passions. What is it that you love doing? Where is it that you love being? What brings you joy? What makes you feel inspired while you are doing it?

_____

_____

_____

_____

_____

_____

_____

_____

_____

_____

_____

_____

#5 is a great place to live. It may be guided by #2, inspired by #1 and #3, and stifled by #4.

Your goal is to live and work in #5 as much as possible. Your truth is the reason you exist. Those are the gifts you've been given and are hopefully, inspired to share with the world. That is the space you will be creating from this point forward.

_____

_____

_____

_____

_____

_____

_____

_____

_____

_____

_____

CHAPTER 7:

CLARITY:
PURPOSE, PASSION AND VALUES

> *The two most important days in your life are the day you were BORN and the day you find out WHY.*
> *—Mark Twain*

love this quote by Mark Twain. We are often "seeking". Seeking what's next, what's new, what's different, what's the same, what's more. We are looking for answers to something and we often feel like something is missing, but can't really put our finger on it. And, in that seeking, we often look to others to define us. We ask for their opinions of our actions or our plans for *our* life. We look outside of ourselves for the answers that we hold inside. This may be because we don't trust ourselves or because we know the answer, but don't like it! So, understanding ourselves and taking responsibility for the outcomes is an essential part of this process.

When we understand ourselves and make decisions based on our truth, we make self-serving choices that do not require outside opinions. The reason these outside-of-us opinions don't work is because they are colored with others' experiences, judgments, and stories that rarely supports our needs.

So, we float along. Living someone else's desires for us, or living *their* dreams or worse, living *their* fears.

Think about the parent that wants you to go to law school or med school. So, you go and you work hard. And you excel. And, you graduate, maybe even with honors. And, you get hired by your dream law firm. And, you put in the hours and the effort and you excel. And, five years later you realize you hate your job…and you don't even know how you got here!

Or, the parent who is so afraid of you leaving to go to college, that you never go. Their fears, their experiences, their dreams (or lack of) become your path.

One day, after much discontent and restlessness, you may feel frustrated, lost, and insecure. Or, you may begin seeking your "why" or your "what's next".

Actually, the only way to overcome living someone else's life or a life on auto-pilot, taking whatever comes along, is to understand your desires, passion, purpose clearly.

The great news is that YOU hold the key. You always have. You hold the answers inside and they reside in your purpose and your passion. So, let's explore.

Heaven knows it wasn't you who set me free
So oftentimes it happens that we live our life in chains
And we never even know we have the key.
—lyrics from "Already Gone" by The Eagles

Your Why - Your Purpose

Your purpose should get you up in the morning, drive your actions, keep you from giving up, and give you direction and inspiration. Your purpose is your why and your why is your purpose. It comes from a deep place in your soul. It is the light in the darkness. Your purpose is too important to ignore. It may be the most important aspect of the process.

As you move forward in this book, your purpose will be your guiding star. It will keep on the right track. It will align your Vision (your dream) with your actions and will use your *passions* as fuel on the path to realization of your life your way.

What is the difference between your why and your passion? How do you get to your why?

Your passion results from your why. Sometimes, you can get to your why from the passion. Sometimes the why is known and the passion results from that knowing.

In corporate Strategic Planning sessions, I work with the business executives to find their way back to the WHY of the business. According to Simon Sinek, author of <u>Start with Why</u>, "People don't buy what you do. They buy *why* you do it." He further explains that we make decisions emotionally, which is the reason explaining your "why" in business is so important. It is the *authenticity* in their (our) story. It's their (our) reason for doing what we do.

I go a step further and write it out loud. Everyone has a *why*, a purpose for his or her life. How our *why* is fulfilled is as individual as our why. It may be fulfilled through our home life, our education, our business, or our way of being. I believe there is a higher purpose for each of us. That is what we are seeking when we are looking for the meaning of life. We are looking for *why* we exist. We know there is something more…we just know it, but can't yet define it—probably because we are looking for the answers from the outside-in instead of the inside-out. Well, the same holds true for life and business, our vision, our dreams come from our purpose. And the fulfillment of that vision serves our higher purpose.

UNCOVERING YOUR PURPOSE EXERCISE

Explaining our *why*: One easy step, if you are creating this for your business, is to start with your *what* and your *how*, so you don't confuse them as your *why.* The *why* is what's left.

Please remember that your why is not the money. You may have determined a method to make money by doing *what* you love, but your *why* is deeper.

1. Define *what* you do: "I write books."

_____

_____

_____

_____

_____

_____

_____

_____

_____

_____

2. Define *how* you do it: "I create the outline, then schedule the time to write. I re-write the chapters until they flow. I send it to the editor. I create the distribution channels and marketing plan. The book is printed for distribution." What's your How? Write it in the space provided.

_____

_____

_____

_____

_____

_____

_____

_____

_____

_____

_____

_____

_____

3.   Define *why* you do it: "Because words matter. And we as women deserve to believe the truth that we are enough; that we are valuable and worthy; that we were born perfect and will always have the power to change our lives. All it takes is a word, or a sentence, or a book to remind us of these truths. And knowing that each *Aha* moment that occurs changes the world".

Write your "Why" below. Remember, this is deeper than money. It brings your *purpose* to life.

_____

_____

_____

_____

_____

_____

_____

_____

_____

_____

_____

_____

Next, let's get to your passion, your heart—that which drives (or should be driving) you.

Your Passion

Your passion comes from deep down inside. It is born of your WHY. There are entire books dedicated to defining your passion—it is *that* important. When I ask clients about their passion, I get a lot of shoulder shrugs. I get the same response when I ask about their dreams. "I don't know", they say. Or "I'm not sure. I like a lot of things."

The truth is that you *do* know your passion. It either scares you to death, you don't believe it serves your life, you don't believe it serves you financially, or worse, someone told you it was stupid or invalid, so you buried it.

I urge you to get a shovel and start digging it out. Let's put your passion on paper. Remember, don't judge your answers...just write.

DEFINING YOUR PASSION EXERCISE

1. What do you love to do? What is it that when you are doing it, time flies and you feel like you could do it all day every day? Your answer may include multiple activities.

2. What do you love doing at work, at school, in everyday life? If money was no issue, describe your ideal job, ideal life. Remember, money is no issue. What would you be doing day in and day out?

_____

_____

_____

_____

_____

_____

_____

_____

_____

_____

_____

_____

_____

3. What fun, knowledge-seeking, spiritual or other activities would you participate in if you had extra time and extra money?

_____

_____

_____

_____

_____

_____

_____

_____

_____

_____

_____

_____

_____

_____

My passions are learning, giving back to the world, self-growth, researching, and teaching. If I look backward, I can see it clearly. I love reading. I've read thousands of books in my lifetime. I can spend hours at conferences learning. In recent years, I have found that being able to teach and motivate others, providing them with life-changing insight and learning, brings me peace and a happy heart. And, from every client, every speaking engagement, every person I encounter, I also learn. It is a great blessing. So, what is your Passion?

Now, let's move into discovering your values and how they matter to your living your dreams.

Your Values

Why are we discussing values? Our values drive our beliefs and judgments. Or, our beliefs and judgments create our values. Understanding your values, how they were created and how you use them daily, will provide more insight into your actions and what drives us in the background. From there, we can decide how they serve our needs. Because it is important to understand where our beliefs and judgments originate. Oftentimes, it is from our value system.

Let's start with the dictionary definition of **values**. From Webster's:

Values: a person's principles or standards of behavior; one's judgment of what is important in life.

Your values are often unconsciously created through your upbringing, your experiences, your challenges, your friends, etc. Understanding them and knowing how they operate in your life is vital to your growth, your story, and your choices.

Your values help you determine if your life is turning out as expected. Understanding your values provides insight into whether the key areas of your life feel connected, aligned, peaceful. They guide your relationships; they direct how you raise children; they show up in how you run your business. And, when your life and your behaviors do not align with your values, you may feel disconnected, unfulfilled, unsettled. Understanding your values will help you on the path to writing your new story.

Let's discuss first how *our values* become *our values*…and what to do with them.

As an example, my most important value is Respect: respect of self and respect for others. It is a value that drives my behaviors—behaviors that serve me and, yes, behaviors that do not serve me or anyone else. It is a value that "provides understanding" of the world around me. It is a judgment tool that allows me to make decisions and choices.

What do you think happens when my most important value, *respect,* is stepped on?

Well, my calm, introspective, open-hearted, loving, respectful "self" disappears! My ego-driven "self" shows up to set everyone straight. My *value* becomes destructive. It is no longer a guide, but instead becomes a sword.

A better question might be: "*Why* is Respect such a strong value for me?"

My insightful answer is: Because as a child I felt powerless, misunderstood, and ignored. However, in the world I saw and the books I read, a belief was created. A belief that *power* and *success* came from *respect*. And, the belief that if I was to gain respect, I had to give it. If I was to *be* respected, I had to command it! Yes, you guessed it…"commanding it" didn't work out too well.

Respect as a value, however, can and does serve my purpose. It allows me to respect others, respect myself and to meet others wherever they are on their journey. Respect for self and others comes from me and me only. As I respect myself, I can respect others. When I feel "disrespected" and react strongly, that is a function of my insecurities, fears, and ego. However, if someone is disrespectful *towards* me, I get to choose the space they are allowed to occupy in my life.

This example illustrates why the "awareness" of our values is so important. My value of respect, when used in the light, to serve my purpose, provides guidance into how to serve others and how to treat others in service of my desire to have meaningful impact. However, a value operating in the darkness, unchecked, becomes an obstacle on our path to the realization of our Vision, our Dreams.

We need to both define our values, and understand how they operate in our everyday life. Then, as we define our story, we can consciously define it in alignment with our values, to ensure our values support our vision.

RECOGNIZING YOUR VALUES EXERCISE

Think about what drives your behaviors. Is there a reaction to how someone talks to you? What about your reaction to someone with money or someone without money?

Think about what motivates your fears? Oftentimes, this comes from your values system. Values can serve us or they can create judgment.

Identify times where you were happiest. What was going right?

What were you doing?

How were people responding?

_____

_____

_____

_____

_____

_____

_____

_____

Next, identify significant choices you've made. What helped you define them? What was most important in the decision process?

_____

_____

_____

_____

_____

_____

_____

_____

_____

_____

_____

_____

_____

Identify judgment of others and self. Identify some of the judgments you have of yourself. Are they similar to the judgments of others? Do you judge based on someone's weight, education, looks, shoes, good enough, kind enough, color of skin, color of eyes? These insights may provide a glimpse into where your values reside.

Write them below.

_____

_____

_____

_____

_____

_____

_____

_____

_____

_____

_____

Here are some Values that will help your thought process along the way:

Achievement	Adventure	Affection	Authenticity
Authority	Balance	Beauty	Competitiveness
Collaboration	Creativity	Empathy	Fame
Family	Happiness	Financial	Freedom
Friendship	Fun	Health	Honesty
Inner Peace	Integrity	Inclusion	Independence
Intelligence	Leadership	Learning	Loyalty
Openness	Order of Things	Persistence	Personal Development
Pleasure	Power	Purpose	Recognition
Reliability	Respect	Responsibility	Self-Care
Self-Development	Solitude	Spirituality	Timeliness
Wealth	Wisdom		

Which of these Values drive your life, your success, your actions? What do the chosen values represent?

Value	What the Value Represents

Value	What the Value Represents

What insights have you gained from understanding your Values? Do your values serve you? Do they serve others? How so?

_____

_____

_____

_____

_____

_____

_____

_____

_____

_____

_____

_____

_____

How will awareness of your values serve your vision? What will change? What will remain the same?

_____

_____

_____

_____

_____

_____

_____

_____

_____

_____

_____

_____

_____

CHAPTER 8

DREAM BIG:
WHAT IS THE STORY YOU WISH TO TELL?

> *Be fearless in the pursuit of what sets your soul on fire.*
> —*Anonymous*

y hope is that:

- You are beginning to see the role of your choices, your beliefs, your thoughts in your life as it is today.
- The beliefs you hold so dear, drive your thoughts, words, actions or inaction.
- You came to these beliefs, mostly unconsciously, through your experiences, outside influence's words, actions, and beliefs.
- Our story, as we tell it, creates the lens through which we see the world and our life and our business.

And, that we wrote the story we tell today, unconsciously and without purpose.

Today, let's write the story we *want* to tell. Let's write the vision for our life and business as we wish for it to be—as we *know* it is capable of being. Write it from your powerful voice. The *voice you have locked away* all these years. Write it from love, not fear. Write it from possiblilty, not from limitation. Write it from the truth that you are a powerful, creative, resourceful, capable, limitless being, put on this earth to discover your greatness.

What would your story be if you were truly living the life of your dreams? What would your business be like if you were operating from a belief of limitless success and abundance? What is the impact on your self? Your family? Your clients? The community? The world?

Make your new story as big and bold as you want it to be. Do not judge it as too big or too small. Allow it to unfold from your truth of unlimited possibility and *knowing* you possess the key. Do not judge it as unattainable.

On the other hand, be aware of these limiting beliefs as they creep into your writing. This is an awareness opportunity. Write these thoughts in your journal. Take your time on this writing journey.

Take three deep cleansing breaths before you start. Write in the present tense. Don't use, "I hope to," or "in the future." Instead, start with "I am". Use prayer, meditation, or any other clarifying exercise that works for you to open your heart and your mind.

So, what this next assignment is asking you to do is to write your story honestly, based on *your* truth of your brilliance, resourcefulness, capability, ability, and possibility of living your life your way. Take the judgment (and limiting beliefs) out of it and just write boldly, out loud, from the inside-out, and in awareness of this moment and your ability to create from possibility!

NEW STORY EXERCISE

Write your new story as you *know* it can be—in your fearless voice and power. Write it as actually happening. It is not only your story, but your vision of what you want your life to be. Don't worry about the "how" to get there—

that is what the Strategy section is all about. For now, we are SheDefining our story.

Write from the knowledge, the "knowing" of:

I AM a powerful woman, destined and created for greatness. I "get to" define my life my way from my truth and inner knowing of the brilliance of my light. I choose today to take the power back from anyone whom I've given it away to and from that place, write the story I wish to tell of the life I choose to lead. And, it starts now, in blessing, gratitude, and peace.

Some housekeeping:

1. Remember, this is *your* story. It requires no approval from any other person on this earth.

2. You are responsible for owning it. This story should serve no one else other than you. The outcome may indirectly serve others, but the story and the resultant life is yours.

3. Your story. Your choices. Your life.

My favorite place to start is with this question:

What would you attempt to do if you knew you could not fail?

Gut check your new story:

1. Does it align with your why, your purpose and your values? Understanding this is key. Does it align with your passion, purpose, and values? Frequently we write from need versus from purpose. So, if we are struggling financially, we may write solely from a financial perspective or even from lack, from fear. Just notice.

2. Does your new story serve your purpose; drive your passion? Are you excited by it? Is it compelling enough to get you up and going on your worst day?

3. Can you see it unfolding? Do you believe it can happen? If not, why not? Again...just notice. No judgment. Only loving kindness towards your "self".

This new story is your story. This begins the process of creating it. Strategy will be the recipe for success. Mindset will be the secret sauce with awareness being the special ingredient.

Are you ready to create? Let's go!

SECTION 3

SHE STRATEGY:
HOW TO GET FROM WHERE YOU ARE TO WHERE YOU WANT TO GO

> *Commitment is the sum of Dreams + Action. Without Action, no dream will ever be fulfilled.*

have spent 10+ years creating Strategic Plans for companies with revenues in the range of $10 - $100 million. The reason companies use strategic plans is to guide the company and the behaviors and actions of its employees. Many of these companies have seen growth in revenues of 40%. Others, have seen growth in market share. Goals have been met and visions have been realized—when the actions aligned with the plan.

A great strategic plan, that is both realistic AND aligned with the Vision of the company is a great tool for goal-getting and growth. However, even the best Strategic Plan without strategic execution (focused action), is worth less than the paper it is written on.

This Section—Creating your She Strategy, uses similar tools to assist you in developing the Plan for getting from where you are today to where you want to go (your Vision, your new story). Because, without action, no dream or goal can be accomplished. And, without focused action, the wrong goals may be realized.

Let's dive into Section 3. Let's get our feet wet. Let go of any preconceived notions about Strategic Planning. This is a She Strategy. It incorporates who we are with what we desire. Our why will drive the actions we take, and the journey, which may or may not look exactly like we plan, will be worth it.

I can't wait to be on this journey with you. Let's go!

CHAPTER 9:

DREAMS REQUIRE A PLAN

When it is obvious that the goals cannot be reached, don't adjust the goals, adjust the action steps.
—Confucius

Maybe you are thinking: "I've tried all this...it just didn't work." I hope so because an awareness opportunity is created. So often we focus on outcomes, and not on the truth of why we are where we are. Instead, ask yourself :

- What is really stopping me from achieving my goals?

- Why do I continue to create chaos and dissatisfaction when I want peace and happiness?

- What do I need to change to be who I want to be in this world?

- What mindset must I have?

- What beliefs must I possess?

- What thoughts are required?

- What actions must I take?

- What is really stopping me from achieving my goals?

- Why do I continue to create chaos and dissatisfaction?

- What do I need to change to be who I want to be in this world?

- What mindset must I have?

- What thoughts do I need to think?

- What actions do I need to take?

The answers are simple, but not easy. You have to desire this change, this "life" so much that you are willing to do *whatever it takes* to achieve it. I promise, all the information, books, knowledge, advice, education in the world will not move you forward into action. Only you can do that. Only you can choose and forge your path forward—intentionally, purposefully, and strategically. Starting from where you are today. Armed with a sense of power, purpose and a plan.

At times you will need to move mountains. You will need to push past those ingrained limiting beliefs that encourage you to sleep in, take breaks, give yourself a pass, and take the easy way out. You will have to dig deeper to arrive at an understanding of what causes self-sabotage, quitting, walking (or running) away.

The truth is, we've all set goals. We've even achieved some of our goals. How many times did you get the exact outcome you set out to get? How often was the outcome exactly as you had hoped or expected? Often when we don't achieve our goals, it was because our goals were based on a lack of substance, purpose, and inner desire. They were goals set without the awareness we've discussed at length in this workbook. Or they were goals set without a focus on their achievement—a plan without focused action and measures for success.

Remember, we create that on which we focus. So, if you were focused on *lack (not enough)* then you got more lack. If you focus on what didn't happen last time you set a goal, then you got more of "what didn't happen". You have to be conscious of your thoughts, your actions, and your attention (energy). A shift in energy will shift everything. A change in beliefs can change a relationship. Shifts in awareness open opportunities everywhere you look.

"How do you want your life to look? " I asked. "Describe it in detail," I continued. "I want to be rich and skinny," my client said.

Okay. What is it that you *really* want? If your desire is to to be rich and skinny, ask yourself what is it that you are trying to be, to feel, to experience? By being rich, are you trying to experience freedom from bills, worrying about money, peace in your financial well-being? "Peace," she said. "I want to not worry about having enough money for retirement. I want to be able to shop freely." "Why?" I asked. "Why do you want more stuff?" "I don't know," she said. "It makes me happy."

"I. Don't. Know." are the three most dangerous words in this process. When you act from *I don't know*, you are moving away from your vision and giving away all your power to create and live the story your desire. *I don't know* creates an unconsciously defined life and the opposite of what you are trying to achieve. Part of the success of this process is the knowing, the clarity, the defining, the stating out loud. *Knowing* what you want and why you want it is as important to your success as declaring it out loud and heartfelt.

On the other hand, "I don't know" represents the opposite. When your answer is I don't know, please use that as a flag to reflect, understand, and address your feelings. Your ability to get to *I know, I want,* and *I am willing to do what it takes* changes the game; shifts the energy; fulfills dreams.

Your "why" is key to understanding what it is you *truly* want and desire. Otherwise, you will continue down the path of what you think you want or what you've come to believe you deserve, versus traveling down the path of what you *truly* want and desire.

If you get in the car without a why, a where, and a how, you will never reach your destination. You may take some interesting detours, but you will end up driving in circles. You may meet interesting people, experience new things, see some great sights, but you will soon run out of gas—never arriving to your undefined destination!.

However, when you get in the car armed with your why, your where, and your how, you will get to the final destination through a map and focused effort. When our purpose is stronger than life's curve balls we can always find our way back to the purposeful path that drives mindset, actions, inspiration, and the ultimate destination: realization of your dreams.

If you are there, then you are ready for what is next...this is the secret sauce!

Taking Action - Developing your SheStrategy

You've got your Vision, your Purpose, your Passion, and your Values. But how will we get to the vision—the SheDefined Story you've written?

The answer is simple: take action. No goal is ever achieved without it. But it can't be just any activity. We must take strategic action—focused, intentional, and purposeful action.

"So," you ask "with all those bright, shiny objects out there, how will I get to my intended vision? How will I stay on track?"

The good news is, it is not complicated. It may not be easy, but it also does not need to be complicated:

1. Create the plan that directly supports your new story—your intended outcome.

2. Take daily strategic (focused intentional) action on the plan

3. Be willing to make changes or shift the plan when needed

4. Be patient!

So, maybe your story, your vision, is this big, beautiful, soul-serving story. It may incorporate many aspects of your life or maybe you constructed your vision around your business only or personal life only. There is no right or wrong. In either case, the next step is to determine what steps must be taken to get to that vision. And, sitting on the couch or surfing the internet, may not serve this vision!

Instead, every day you get to ask yourself:

"Is what I'm doing today moving me closer to or further away from my goals?"

And, then, get back on task if the answer is "further away from". Your plan, that we will create from here, is your roadmap from where you are today to where you soul is pushing you to be. Let's create the plan to move you forward in the direction of your dreams.

To complete your 1-page SheStrategy plan please go to:

www.SheDefined.com/She-Strategy-the-Book

CHAPTER 10:

PLANS REQUIRE ACTION

> *Dream. Decide. Do.*

've created Strategic Plans for companies from the Start-up stage up to $100 Million companies. And, the process is the same.

In the process of planning is where the clarity is gained, and a focused action plan can be developed. When clarity, focus, and action is combined, a strategic plan is born.

She Strategy, however, also includes all the work we did in the first 2 sections of the book. She Strategy incorporates mindful, intentional, on-purpose visioning and planning. She Strategy considers you as a whole person and starts from where you are.

So, you've done all the hard work by looking in the mirror and becoming accountable to your Vision. You are ready to "own the outcome".

This final section moves you into planning for the fulfillment and unfolding of the Vision for your life your way.

Developing Your SheStrategy

Your Strategy for your Success

And, now it is your turn. You've done the work on your *self*. You know you have choices and you *get to* define this next chapter of your life or business. You've discovered what's holding you back and gained some tools to drive your life forward. And, from here is where we start to go forward with clarity, focus your efforts, and take meaningful steps toward living your dream.

We start with creating the recipe, the road map, from where you are today to where you want to go—it is your *Strategy for Success.*

I know what you are thinking: How can this be relevant for my business or for my life, you ask. Isn't Strategy a business concept?

So, yes, Strategy is a business concept, however, the concept of Strategy is relevant to living life, as well. The dictionary definition of strategy is "a plan of action designed to achieve a major or overall aim or goal". Think about how that can be applied to both business and life. This next section takes what is a complex process in corporate America and breaks it down into simple, relevant, and meaningful steps to help you build either (or both)—the life or business of your dreams. The life and business that you say you want to live!

So, what is SheStrategy?

SheStrategy begins with awareness of self, and awareness of the power you possess in this moment and keeps you focused on your dreams, your vision for your life, the success of your business and has the power to move you forward, through fears and into your innate power to live the life of your dreams of your choosing. SheStrategy supports and aligns with your purpose and provides clear directions on how to live the life, business, success you desire.

SheStrategy is intended to keep you going in the right direction, when there are so many other options and opportunities—when there are so many other bright, shiny objects vying for your attention.

Are you ready? Let's go!

Success Factors of Your Strategy

KYSS- Keep your Strategy Simple
Strategy should be simple. Remember, "If you can't explain it simply, you don't understand it well enough"

Simple – is straightforward and supports *your* vision *your* way

Meaningful – your strategy must align with your purpose, passion, values, and dreams—as you have defined them

Clear - Easy to communicate. Driving your dreams is not complicated if you are clear on where you are going. Your strategy should be easy to explain, align with your purpose, and have a well-defined path so you can consistently and purposefully act daily to move you forward in the direction of your dreams!

Starting Place: Your Vision Your Dream

> **If your dreams don't scare you, they are not big enough.**

This next exercise requires you to be in the mindset of infinite possibility. Use your meditation, prayer or awareness exercises to let go of thoughts of the past, and open yourself to this moment and the truth of infinite possibility that has been granted to you, through your birth.

DREAMS EXERCISE

Step 1: Define the overall Vision, based on your NEW story, for your plan. This is your guiding star. This is your lighthouse in the storm, when you move into fear or limiting beliefs. It needs to get you up in the morning and bring you back to focus when you are distracted, fearful, or ready to give up.

It can be one or two sentences.

Ask yourself: Where do I want to go? Who do I want to be? What is the *ultimate* outcome that I desire? What is my greatest dream for my life or my business?

Remember when we discussed the "story" you wished to tell. Think back to *your* story. Ensure that your Vision aligns with and supports your story, your values. As you write this, do it from a peaceful place. Feel it. Does it feel in-flow or does it feel forced? Are you thinking too small? Are you judging your dream or holding back at all? This is *your* dream; *your* vision for *your* life. Do not hold back—this is the key to your success.

Sometimes, this process of getting to clarity and stating our dreams is the most difficult. We are so afraid to acknowledge our dreams. We fear the scorn and judgement of others. We judge it as not attainable. Our "not good enough" thoughts will come up and try to take over. Our "I don't have the money, the intelligence, the network, the relationship, the environment, the support, the time" thoughts will creep in.

Remember to use your tools from the first half of this book to get into the present moment, bring awareness, and let those limiting thoughts (the lies) go. Try not to engage in those thoughts and beliefs that have held you back. Instead shift into the truth of who you are and for now focus just on the dream; not on how you are going to attain it.

Let's get started. Use the following prompt, if you are stuck

When your vision (your story) is accomplished, what is the outcome?

To give you an example, SheDefined's Vision is:
A world where every woman knows her worth and uses her innate power and her authentic voice to build success and live her life on her terms.

"What would your life be like if all your dreams came true? Describe that! Let your thoughts flow—uncensored. Just write.

_____

_____

_____

_____

_____

_____

_____

_____

_____

_____

_____

_____

And now, define in one to two sentences, from your journaling, your overall Vision that will guide your Strategy. This is your Strategic Vision. This can be more specific, aligned with your overall vision—it will guide your goals. She-Defined's Strategic Vision is: To create impactful programs through coaching, training, and retreats to serve thousands of women annually, throughout the world.

_____

_____

_____

_____

_____

_____

_____

_____

_____

_____

_____

SETTING STRATEGIC GOALS
FOR YOUR BUSINESS OR LIFE

Starting with your Strategic Vision, let's define the goals required to support the outcome of your vision. These can be short-term or long-term, but we recommend starting with short-term, for practice.

A lesson about goals.

Goals must drive intentional, focused action. To do that, a goal must be S.M.A.R.T.

Specific

Your goal must be clearly stated with specific outcomes. Goals must not be vague. It is impossible to accomplish a vague goal.

An example of a "vague" goal is: To get healthy

This vague goal provides no direction on your path. "Get healthy" can have hundreds of meanings and may have different meanings to you today than it will tomorrow.

Instead, an example of a "specific" goal is: To lose 20 pounds by March 1st. This gives you a clear goal to help you take focused action. And, must align with and support your overall Vision

Measurable

A goal must have a measurement of success to determine if your action is resulting in the outcomes you require; and to provide insight into whether you need to shift your actions to shift the results. Also, without measurability, how will you know if you ever attained your goal

Example of a Measurable Goal: Grow the company's revenues by $200,000

Example of a Non-measurable Goal: Grow the company's revenues (this may be specific, but it is not measurable)

Accountable

Accountable means that some person is responsible for the successful outcome of the goal by a specific date. However, it is still your responsibility to hold them accountable to both the outcome and the agreed upon date for completion

There may be many goals where your name is the accountable name – and that is okay. Don't let this overwhelm you. Your goals are going to light the path for your daily actions. This is good news!

Relevant and Realistic

Your Goals must support and align with your Strategic Vision. They must be relevant to what you wish to achieve.

Additionally, the goals need to be realistic. If your goals is to earn $1,000,000 in 3 months when you are making $20,000 today, you may need to set a more realistic goal or timeline.

Timebound

Your goals need to have a due date or a date of accomplishment. This date is to guide your actions, so you can manage your time. It is not so that you can beat yourself up for not hitting the deadline. It is okay to move the date, when needed, however ensure it is not a moving target.

Let's Practice:

- **What are some short-term goals? Remember, they must be Specific, Measurable, Accountable, Realistic, Timebound?**

- **What are the behaviors or actions that you will take to directly influence the outcome of those goals?**

GOAL SETTING EXERCISE

1. Recount your Strategic Vision. Write it at the top of each Goal Sheet.

2. Write one of your goals. Define how it is specific and measurable. Define how it aligns with and supports the vision.

3. To make it an *accountable* goal, write the name of the person responsible for its successful completion. Also, note the agreed upon date for accomplishment. Then make sure you use that date to check-in and ensure the goal is on target.

Specific, Measurable Goal	Aligns with Vision?
Measurement of Success	**Accountable/Date**

This and all the following journal pages can be downloaded in full PDF version by visiting our website at www.SheDefined.com/She-Strategy-the-Book

Focused effort is required for success. Focused effort that directly supports your Vision is required for realization of your Vision.

In this next worksheet, you will take one of the goals written in the last exercise and write it at the top of each Goal Sheet. And, for this specific goal, write out the Tasks or Activities that must happen (daily, weekly or monthly) to attain the SMART goal, as written. This is your focused action list.

What are the behaviors or actions that you will take to directly influence the outcome of those goals?

GOAL:

Action/Behavior	Intended Outcome	Time Interval /Date	Measurement of Success

What Stops Us?

Risks to our Success Section

Life happens. We got to where we are today based on the experiences we've had, lessons we've learned (or not), and the choices we have made. Many, many choices. Those choices result from the beliefs and thoughts generated from our experiences. It is a cycle of experiences, thoughts, beliefs, actions, and choices. Take a minute to consider that cycle and how it plays out in your life, your family, and your professional world.

In this section, I would like you to consider and acknowledge any risks, obstacles or roadblocks to this great vision; to your destined life. Write them down. Acknowledge that they exist. Own that they are a part of who you are today, and that they may rear their ugly heads during this process.

These risks and obstacles may be fears, financial concerns, life-work balance needs, family requirements, beliefs, thoughts and insecurities, outside influences, health—you name it! Essentially, they are fears. Fears with only one intention—to hold you back from your greatness.

We are bringing these fears to light because only in awareness and acknowledgment can there be change.

Overcoming the Risks

The other part of this exercise is defining the potential steps to overcome these "risks" to your success. Do this from a mindset of *possibility*. What are the opportunities for overcoming the obstacles? What mindset work can you do to create a habit of fearless thoughts and beliefs. What conversations MUST you have to ensure your family has clarity of your intentions? What do you need to do to ensure your truth guides your intentions?

This is where a coach or mentor may be instrumental to your growth in this process. Don't hesitate to ask for help on this path. This is a key success factor of successful women – asking for help when it is needed. You do not have to do this alone, even if that is the only way you've ever done it!

Remember, the success of your life is dependent on you. Be open to the beauty of the path. Develop an inner dialogue of progress, not perfection. Let go of all that does not serve you, use your authentic voice. Allow for "what is" to exist without approval, but with acceptance. From there, let's understand our self-imposed barriers and let's knock them down, one by one.

OVERCOMING OBSTACLES EXERCISE

This exercise should be done on different days. Step 1 is Day 1. Step 2 is Day 2.

They each take different mindsets, so be okay with not rushing through this.

Day 1/Step 1: Define the barriers to your success. Define them one by one. You may feel like there are too many to list. Don't judge. Just write. We ALL have risks and obstacles to overcome…let the judgments go.

_____

_____

_____

_____

_____

_____

_____

_____

_____

_____

Day 2/Step 2: What are the options to mitigating the risk and overcoming the barrier? Do this part on a different day from the day you write the obstacles. Take some time to become very present and aware. Write your solutions from a mindset of the truth of your power. From the mindset of possibility!

And, remember, you don't have to do any of this alone. Reach out to a She Defined coach or someone you know who uplifts and supports your dreams from a healthy mindset of love!

Risks to Your Success

Obstacles, Fears, Roadblocks	Steps to Overcome These Risks
Example: Not enough money to get started	Define clearly what is needed to get started financially. Set expectations and a budget. Make simple changes in spending habits.

This dream, this vision, this plan will take commitment. Commitment is hard work. Commitment is taking action even when you don't feel like it. Commitment is taking action even when you can find a million excuses (good ones even) why you can't.

There is a difference between trying hard and committing to a goal. When we use the word try, as in "I tried, it didn't work" or "I'll try" we open the door for excuses and reasons why we "can't". When we truly commit, there are no excuses. There is just action.

Think about a time you committed to something…anything. Maybe it was conscious, maybe it wasn't. Let's take an easy one. How committed are you to your dental health? Do you get up every day and brush and floss? Do you brush again before going to bed? If so, you are "committed", even if it is not conscious.

I'll give you an example of a personal commitment. I am "committed" to being healthy. One of my goals is getting to the gym 3 days a week at 5 AM, because I know for me and my schedule, that is the best time to go. However, and it is a big however, it is difficult to get out of bed at 5 AM, even though it is only 20 minutes earlier than my regular time! So, I was not going to the gym. I "tried" to get up, but just couldn't. I was tired. I was working too hard. I deserved to sleep in. The excuses were many!

Through my coach, I realized that I was not actually committed to getting healthy. Instead, I was unconsciously committing to sleep, which is not bad or wrong, it is just a competing commitment. And, once I realized that commitment can be unconscious, as well, I started to become aware of my actual commitment and how they aligned with (or did not align with) my goals and vision.

And, that is what I request of you. Look deep. What are you committed to on the journey? How important is this dream of yours? What are you willing to do? Who are you willing to be?

Once you are truly committed, taking strategic action, aligned with your goals, will move you forward.

To download the One Page Strategy Plan go to:
www.SheDefined.com/she-strategy-the-book

SheDefined™ ONE PAGE SUCCESS PLAN

VISION / DREAM

WHY / PURPOSE

GOALS:

TASKS (Focused Activities that Support the Goals)

RISKS

COMMITMENT STATEMENT

CHAPTER 11:

ACTION REQUIRES FOCUS

> *Who you are, what you think, feel, and do, what you love—is the sum of what you focus on.*
> —*Cal Newport*, Deep Work: Rules for Focused Success in a Distracted World

When you are ready to take action, the tools of our modern world will distract you. You'll be magnetically drawn to your phone, your email, your lunch, or that productivity tool you're dying to check out (to see if it works!). Your list of distractions will be impressive. You are not alone.

While I was writing this paragraph, I stopped to check my email, looked up a hotel for my daughter's graduation party, checked my phone because I had an upcoming call and wanted to see if I missed it, and then got up to get a bottle of water. All while writing this one paragraph. I am not kidding.

So, how do we get around all this? How do we shift into *focused effort*? How do we create a specific time to do a specific task that will help bring about our new life story? What if I told you I don't have an answer? You'd probably throw this book across the room!

I do have some answers—not just one! A lot will depend on where you are and what you are willing to do. But, before we get into that, I want to explain more fully why focused effort (some call it deep work) actually works. There is scientific research related to distraction versus focused effort—and—there is my direct experience along with the experience of hundreds of thousands of others who have reaped the benefits of Focused Effort.

Focus lights the path. Focus is big, bright, stadium lights on your path. Now, whether you choose to go down the well-lit path is up to you. But, if you are clear on where you want to go…then the next step is *how* you are going to get there. We know it may not be a straight, direct line to success. When we are focused on the path, even the bends, the curves, the cracked sidewalks, the hills, are all manageable. A well-lit path of planning and focused effort brings you back to the path whenever you get distracted.

Your focus, your commitment, and your passion are what lights the way.

First, what causes the distraction?

Fear

Yes, fear. Fear of "what if". Fear of the unknown. Fear of failure. "Heck, if I don't get started, then I can't fail." Fear of not finishing. Fear of getting started. Fear of not knowing how. Fear of criticism. Fear of not being good enough. You get the picture.

Life

Our life gets in the way of living our life. Seems crazy right? But we often use life as an excuse for not having the life we desire.

We have plenty to do, all the time. We can find distraction in email, a co-worker's needs, laundry, a messy house, a messy desk, a child's needs, a spouse's needs, a crisis of any sort…and the list goes on. Many may be valid in the moment; most are not!

And, what does distraction create? Distracted effort and procrastination.

Procrastination

Procrastination is the disease of fear. This disease, without medicine, becomes our unconscious life; the life we live, created from the outside-in instead of from the inside-out.

So, *Focused Effort* is the medicine. And Focused Effort, drives intentional behavior.

Tools for Working from Focused Effort

Back away from the email. Yes, I said it! One of the greatest time-sucks is email. We get "distracted" by what someone else needs in an email and make it an immediate response requirement. We have somehow created a belief in ourselves that we MUST respond to emails immediately to be like, respected, or loved! And, many of us have created the *expectation* that we will respond to an email no matter the time or the circumstances! Okay...maybe it's just me, but if it applies to you, just notice it.

Tool #1: EMAIL SCHEDULING

Schedule time during the day to review emails: 8:00, 11:00 and 3:00. Communicate this to employees, clients, friends, to create the expectation of timely, but not necessarily immediate, response.

Focused Effort required focused (non-distracted) time to work on a specific task. How, do you do this without distraction?

Tool #2: FOCUSED EFFORT SCHEDULING

Schedule (yes, in your calendar) 1-2 hour blocks to work on specific tasks from your Strategic Plan. Non-distracted time means 1) no emails; 2) no phones; 3) no Internet; 4) no kids. It means door closed, head-down work. For some this may mean scheduling throughout the day. For others, it may mean 5 AM or 10 PM work.

These are just a few tools to bring awareness and to get you started. But, if you want more, there are entire books focused solely on Focused Effort!

CHAPTER 12:
THE FINAL STEP: LETTING GO

On this journey of discovery and defining, our passion and our purpose begins to drive our behaviors and our excitement. We have created the plan, are using focused effort and moving our dreams, our vision, forward towards fruition.

Our final step now is to *let go.*

Wait. Give me a minute to explain.

The Tao Te Ching says, "When I let go of who I am, I become who I was meant to be. When I let go of what I have, I receive what I need." And, I will add: When I let go of what I *think* I need, I receive what I'm *meant* to have.

So, in saying "let go", I mean let go of the pre-conceived version of your outcome. Let go of your very specific, "it must look this way" Vision.

Our vision, our dream is ours and our activities are driving us towards it.

However, the unfolding of our Vision may not look exactly as we had expected. Our Vision is vivid and real, so it could feel as if all our hard work isn't paying off if we are blinded only by our one version of the outcome.

When we hold on so tight to our version of success, we don't recognize any other version, and worse, may close up shop, just as our Vision is unfolding.

So, instead, we let go. We "allow" it to unfold. We open our minds. And, as we allow, all our effort becomes a collaboration with the plans of the Universe (or your God). Those plans may be much greater than our own vision, and so we co-create a life we couldn't actually imagine.

Speak up, plan and take action. Then, let go my friends. Open yourself up to all the possibility that exists and be in gratitude for what shows up.

And, live your dreams in more vivid color than you could have ever imagined.

Speaker Program Topics

Program I: Harnessing the Power of Choice
Choices define our lives – both personal and business. Understanding and seeing the choices that have lead us to where we are today and learning to make conscious choices for ourselves and our employees are keys to successful business and successful living.

Program II: How to Fascinate® – Branding our Best Selves
This is an Assessment based, fun, insightful program that is based on the work of Sally Hogshead's branding and communication program How to Fascinate. This assessment provides insight into how "others see us" and how to best use our personal assets to be more successful.

Program III: Strategic Risk Taking to Achieve Success
What stops us from achieving all the success that we are capable of? One word…fear. This program dives deep into understanding the obstacles we put in place and how to overcome them for success at any level.

Custom Programs:
We create custom leadership and coaching programs based on your company's needs. Contact us for more information.

www.SheDefined.com

For more information and
availability call:

(800) 294-5104
Julia@SheDefined.com

To access Author Julia Aquino-Serrano's event schedule and meet her person go to: www.SheDefined.com/events/

Author: Julia Aquino-Serrano

Julia Aquino-Serrano grew up in Hialeah, a suburb of Miami. She was the first in her family to go to college and is a serial entrepreneur, author, speaker, mom, wife, breast cancer survivor, and business coach.

She is currently running three successful companies: SheDefined, Tees for Humanity, and All Systems Grow.

Her unwavering passion is helping women define their vision, clarify their purpose, and find their authentic voice so they can consciously live the life of their dreams, of their choosing.

She helps clients through high-level coaching sessions, retreats, workshops, and speaking forums.

Julia has a diverse business background that includes 25-plus years of hands-on experience in strategic planning, operational management, and leadership development. She has helped dozens of companies shift their collective mindset and change the course of their operations. This has translated into growth, profitability, efficiency, and operational excellence in the small to medium-sized business space.

Julia has a Bachelor of Science in Finance and an MBA, but finds that her most effective tools are her natural leadership skills, her intelligence and warmth, and thanks to her experience raising teenagers, her fearlessness.

She shares part of her story in her first book, *SheStrategy*, and gives us a glimpse into the life experiences and lessons that drives her success and her desire for inner growth and peace.